WEDDING
BOOK

Harrods
KNIGHTSBRIDGE
WEDDING
BOOK

SUE CARPENTER

EBURY PRESS · LONDON

First published by Ebury Press
an imprint of the Random Century Group
Random Century House
20 Vauxhall Bridge Road
London SW1V 2SA

Edited by Alison Wormleighton
Designed by The Image
Picture Research by Gabrielle Allen

British Library Cataloguing in Publication Data
Carpenter, Sue
  Harrods wedding book.
  1. Weddings. Planning
  I. Title
  395.22

  ISBN 0-85223-990-4

Filmset in Monophoto Bembo by Advanced Filmsetters (Glasgow) Ltd.
Printed and Bound in Italy by New Interlitho S.p.a., Milan

Contents

Introduction

The great irony of getting married is that only afterwards do you know how to do it. That's why, as you've probably noticed, so many of your espoused friends and family keep showering you with the fruits of their knowledge. You may also have realised that not all the advice tallies. Besides, you have your *own* ideas. It's a confusing business for the uninitiated. What you need is an impartial arbiter to guide you through the preparations for staging a wedding—which is where the *Harrods Wedding Book* comes in.

The advice and ideas in this book have been culled from the comments of many newlyweds who have been through the traumas and triumphs of organising a wedding, as well as experts who work in the wedding industry—florists, dressmakers, wedding-cake bakers. The result is both a sourcebook of ideas and a highly practical reference guide on every aspect of the wedding arrangements—from selecting an engagement ring and setting the date of the ceremony to deciding on a venue for the reception and choosing the vehicle in which you will be going away. Use the *Harrods Wedding Book* for reference, for inspiration and for reassurance.

Word-of-mouth recommendation is the surest way of selecting your professional wedding helpers. Their role is crucial to the smooth running of the preparations; you need to be sure you can trust them, and that they'll be calm and supportive when you're feeling overwrought. The *Harrods Wedding Book* gives you a head start by providing advice on exactly what criteria to use when evaluating these professionals, from party planners and caterers to photographers and video cameramen.

Tradition and etiquette are wedding watchwords: the event is a formal social occasion and no one wants to make a mistake. This book covers not only the hard-and-fast rules, but the areas where modern manners suggest a little bending of the rules. (Should the groom's family offer to pay for part of the reception? Is it mercenary to have a wedding list? Do you really have to have a receiving line? How risqué should the best man's speech be?) With the *Harrods Wedding Book*, you can be sure that no social blunders will be made.

You can, however, follow tradition without following the crowd. A little flair and originality make a wedding more memorable. Happily, it takes thought, planning and imagination rather than a Swiss bank account, and in this book you will find dozens of ideas for such important aspects of the wedding as music, flowers, food and drink, transport, and entertainment. Harrods stands for quality above all, and this book is not just for those who have cases of vintage champagne waiting in the cellar and the family tiara sitting in the bank vaults, but for everyone who wants a wedding with style and individuality.

RIGHT
Knowing that every detail of your wedding has been carefully planned, you can relax and float through the day in a romantic haze.

On Getting Engaged

AFTER THAT MOMENT OF PURE ROMANCE WHEN HE ASKS YOU TO MARRY HIM, YOU ARE AGLOW WITH HAPPINESS, PARTIES ARE THROWN IN YOUR HONOUR, CARDS OF CONGRATULATION FLOOD IN, YOUR ENGAGEMENT RING IS FLASHED TO ADMIRING FRIENDS AND RELATIONS. BUT IT'S NOT ALL PLAIN SAILING: THE ENGAGEMENT PERIOD FOLLOWS A NATURAL COURSE OF HIGHS AND LOWS. IT'S GOODBYE TO CAREFREE DAYS OF INDEPENDENCE, HELLO TO A DIZZY AND STRESSFUL WHIRL OF ACTIVITY. THIS IS A TIME FOR PLANS AND DECISIONS, FOR ORGANISATION AND DELEGATION.

Proposal and Engagement

Out of fashion in the Seventies, revived in the Eighties, only natural in the Nineties, the formal betrothal involves the proposal of marriage, the acceptance, the announcement (verbally to family and friends, in print to the world if you wish), and the giving of a ring.

Traditionally, the man asks the girl, 'Will you marry me?' and, on her acceptance, goes to see her father, or mother if her father is unavailable, to request his daughter's hand in marriage. The father then consents to give his daughter away. Many men like to stick to this tradition, although they will invariably have discussed marriage with their girlfriends before the actual proposal, and fathers are presented with a fait accompli rather than an option. Some men never actually propose, however—the marriage simply becomes an inevitability, a mutual understanding.

RIGHT

His-and-hers wedding rings are highly favoured among the majority of couples—surveys show that some 80 per cent of husbands like to proclaim their status by wearing a ring.

RIGHT

He has proposed, you have accepted. For a short while you share this secret. Make the most of these moments together before announcing your engagement to the world, when your lives will suddenly become public property.

ANNOUNCING THE ENGAGEMENT

According to a recent survey, the average engagement lasts 20 months. Many men and women need that time to save up for their wedding, honeymoon and future home. Among couples who have the wherewithal to marry when they wish, the average engagement time is cut down to approximately six months—as long as it takes to organise the wedding comfortably.

From the moment you make your engagement public your time is not your own. So do stop and collect your thoughts before telling *anyone*. Then take a deep breath and start telephoning. Parents come first, then close relations and friends. After this, you can make an official announcement in the newspapers, traditionally *The Times* and/or *Daily Telegraph*. It is not wise to give your exact address. It gives rise to the worst sort of bridal shower—from photographers, caterers and the like. However, you will still receive some unsolicited mail from companies that keep nationwide telephone directories.

Some couples choose to place an announcement in the Court and Social pages after the event. Perhaps you have had a quick, quiet wedding, or a grand wedding which you feel deserves further trumpeting. You may include as much or as little detail as you wish. Most local papers carry an editorial page on local weddings. To be considered for inclusion, send a wedding photograph (black-and-white if possible), the name and home town of the bride and groom, the name and place of the church, and the date of the wedding.

BEING ENGAGED

The first priority, if it has not already occurred, is for the parents to meet. This should be arranged on neutral territory—a restaurant, for example. The bride and groom should pay for the event, so that neither set of parents takes the role of the gracious hosts or the grateful guests.

Don't expect life to carry on as normal. From now on, you will be rushed round from one aged aunt to another, and from cakemaker to florist. Both sets of parents will be on the hotline constantly to see how arrangements are going. It is a tense and emotional business, and most brides report a trickle of tears and rows during the lead-up to The Day. Your best defence is to be as organised as possible and to settle major decisions fairly early on. Try to remain cool and unfazed by the inevitable irritations, and enjoy the good aspects: benevolent wishes, presents, and the fact that this is all for you.

Each side of the family may have a small celebration party to introduce the newcomer to relations and friends. The couple may hold their own celebration party for their friends. (One couple had a spontaneous drinks party and pinned the newspaper announcement to their front door by way of explanation.) Parents usually give the couple a token present, and there will be dozens of cards and letters congratulating you.

You may want to have an engagement portrait of you alone, or a joint portrait like the royals have. A good studio will take happy, relaxed portraits which are a lovely informal keepsake for you and the family. (See pages 54–56 for advice on choosing a photographer.)

CHOOSING THE ENGAGEMENT RING

The engagement ring, originally the contractual seal on a betrothal, is a token of love between the couple, and a sign to the outside world that this woman is spoken for. When choosing an engagement ring, bear in mind that it will be worn with a wedding ring (see page 17), so it is a good idea to look at them together, to make sure they complement each other. The ring should be a perfect fit: it is easy to have the ring adjusted. If you can twist it on your finger, it is too big, and the motion will wear the gold down. Clean it regularly to prevent its condition from deteriorating. Dip the ring into hand-hot water with crystal soda, and brush it with a toothbrush. Don't forget to insure your engagement ring as soon as possible.

BUYING A NEW RING

Go to a reputable jeweller. There is no such thing as a bargain: you get no more than you pay for (though if you buy from a non-professional, you may get *less*). Decide on an upper price limit, and ask the jeweller for the very best quality he has in your range. Small stones cost proportionately less than larger ones of the same quality, thus you get more for your money with a cluster than a solitaire. Mass-market modern rings from high-street jewellers tend to be predictable, and the settings can be clumsy and unattractive, though some jewellery chains have a higher standard than others.

ANTIQUE AND SECOND-HAND RINGS

An old ring gives better value for money. What you pay for are the quality and size of stone, not labour. What you get are character, style, individuality,

ABOVE

The Duchess of York's ruby and diamond engagement ring suits her red hair and fiery personality.

superior craftsmanship, a finer cut, a more intricate setting. The metalwork is an intrinsic part of the design and can be as pretty as the stones. Consider a second-hand modern ring too—anything original and hand-crafted. Make sure the stones are secure and the claws in good condition, as repairs can be fairly expensive.

Most antique rings—those over 100 years old—are too delicate for constant wear. From the Edwardian era onwards, rings became more practical, and most 20th century rings are suitable. A ring from the family jewel box (either yours or your fiancé's) is always special. It may have to be altered, restored and cleaned, so take it to a reputable jeweller to do the work. Otherwise, you can scour jewellery shops that specialise in old pieces, antique shops and markets, or investigate the auction rooms.

Look for Victorian rings containing precious stones whose initial letters spell such words as DEAREST (diamond, emerald, amethyst, ruby, epidote, sapphire, turquoise), LOVE ME (lapis lazuli, opal, verd antique, emerald, moonstone, epidote) or REGARD (ruby, emerald, garnet, amethyst, ruby, diamond). Other antique styles to look out for include the carved half-hoop in gold, its sides carved with scrolls, and a row of stones set on top; and the gypsy-set ring, like a wide, tapered wedding ring with stones set into the band. There are also puzzle rings, which should never be removed for fear that the wearer could not complete the ring again—proof then of her infidelity.

Edwardian rings are highly favoured today. Elegant, traditional and well constructed, most tend to have flattish settings that don't catch on clothes. You might find a small, flower-like diamond cluster, three sapphires encircled by tiny diamonds, or a square-shaped ring with a stone in the centre and square-cut stones at the corners. Decorative art nouveau and geometric art deco rings are fabulously stylish, and their rarity makes them a good investment.

HAVING A RING DESIGNED

An engagement (and/or wedding) ring designed to order is particularly special, since it's the only item created for your marriage that you can wear, day in, day out, for the rest of your life. There are a number of talented young individuals who design to order, blending imaginative ideas with fine craftsmanship. They need not be too expensive and are best found through word of mouth. Alternatively, a designer can convert an unwanted piece of jewellery into a ring and other more wearable items—a brooch into a ring and earrings, say.

CHOOSING THE STONES

Naturally, the stones are largely a matter of colour preference and fashion. The majority of girls go for an all-diamond engagement ring, with a solitaire shining out above the rest. The diamond is classic and stylish, ultra-wearable and ultra-durable. On a multi-stoned ring, you will see its sharp facets glinting long after the other jewels have worn smooth. Diamonds really are forever, the word deriving from the Greek *adamas*—impenetrably hard.

Princess Diana's sapphire and diamond cluster was widely copied, and this combination of stones is the second most popular, after the all-diamond ring. The sapphire is an easy-to-wear blue and is very durable, as are garnets, rubies and other less-usual gems. The expensive emerald is easily fractured. Avoid pearls, turquoise, coral, opals and other porous stones which will not stand up to a soaking; pearls can also drop out as they are glued rather than set in a clasp.

Old stones have an iridescence and subtlety of colour that many modern ones cannot match—sapphires are a translucent cobalt blue and rubies a rosy pink, compared to the dark, dull blues and reds of inferior stones available on the high street.

In folklore the stones have a special significance. Sardonyx is said to ensure married happiness, and bloodstone brings courage. Pearls can symbolise tears. The opal—always changing its colours—represents inconstancy in the one who wears it.

The superstitious should also note that to lose or damage an engagement ring bodes ill, lest the bond it represents should suffer. If another girl tries on the ring, the owner's future happiness could be jeopardised.

BIRTHSTONES

An engagement ring containing your birthstone traditionally brings luck. Here are the stones for each month, together with their symbolism.

January	garnet	constancy, truth
February	amethyst	sincerity
March	aquamarine	courage
April	diamond	innocence, light
May	emerald	happiness, success in love
June	pearl	beauty
July	ruby	love, preserves chastity
August	peridot	joy
September	sapphire	wisdom
October	opal	hope
November	topaz	fidelity
December	turquoise	success, prevents matrimonial arguments

CHOOSING THE METAL

All gold is alloyed with other metals to make it more durable. The carat refers to the amount of pure gold per 24 parts. 22-carat gold is almost pure and therefore the most expensive, but it is of less value in a ring as it will wear down sooner than the hardy 18-carat. White gold is 18-carat gold alloyed with silver. Platinum is the most practical metal: it can be made slender, yet is as strong as gold and maintains its whiteness and polish. Choose engagement and wedding rings of the same carat. It is inevitable, however, that the solid

LEFT

Two rings of solid gold. Precious and everlasting, they symbolise the marriage itself, with the circle signifying endless love.

wedding band will wear down the fine underside of an engagement ring. (To avoid this, there is no reason why you shouldn't wear your engagement ring on another finger after you are married.)

THE WEDDING RING

The wedding ring, which dates back to the ancient Egyptians, is placed on the third finger of the left hand because it was thought that this finger carried a vein leading directly to the heart. Made from enduring, ever-valuable gold, it is supposed to bestow upon its wearer a similarly long-lasting and treasured marriage. A wedding ring that is broken or removed is a bad omen.

Almost every couple likes a new wedding ring, or perhaps an inherited one. A plain band of 18-carat gold is the most popular, but don't be afraid of trying something more unusual—a fine double band or an engraved band, say. Many wedding rings today contain gemstones, and engagement and wedding rings may be purchased as a matching pair. Be sure to try the two together for style and fit. A special ring can be made with a crook in it to fit around a large engagement ring.

If the idea of a second-hand wedding ring does not bother you, look for one at auction. Here they sell mainly for bullion unless they have a point of interest such as an inscription or date from the 18th century or earlier. Rings inscribed with poems or love ditties are occasionally available.

A wedding ring is not just for the bride: more and more men wear one these days. Matching pairs for bride and groom are available. If he chooses not to have a ring, you may want to buy him a present of a similarly lasting nature— cufflinks, a watch or gold lighter, for example.

Setting the Date

ABOVE

If you are lucky enough to be able to stage your wedding reception in a garden (or even a field), summer is the ideal season. Little pageboys and bridesmaids certainly enjoy the freedom of outdoor celebrations.

As with all aspects of the wedding, the date is partly a matter of choice, partly one of practicality. The time of year is up to you, but the actual date may not be. Availability—of church, reception venue, photographer and so on—will be a deciding factor. Professionals advise checking their availability before finalising the date.

Some couples want to marry as soon as they can after getting engaged. Organisation of a traditional wedding will take from about three months out of season to six in high season (May to September). Christmas is another busy period, when party services and equipment may be booked up. London weddings may also need extra time, particularly during the party/events seasons (late October to early January; late April to early August). Don't set so tight a deadline that you get overwrought trying to fit everything in.

A WEDDING FOR ALL SEASONS

The quintessential English wedding takes place on a shimmering summer's day, the bride's dress dazzling in the sunlight, guests wandering around a garden awash with colour, every photo a winner against a perfect blue sky. Of course the idea is irresistible, and the vast majority of couples aim for this kind of nuptial nirvana.

However, you don't *have* to follow the expected path. Instead of a summer's afternoon by sunlight, why not a winter's evening by candlelight? Warming mulled wine instead of chilled champagne? Hot sausages and mince pies instead of salmon sandwiches and meringues? Fur-trimmed velvet instead of lace-trimmed silk?

While no amount of advice will sway the confirmed summer bride, the open-minded may like to consider the disadvantages of the high season. First, the weather. If it's hot, there will be the wilting bouquet and sandwiches, and the sweltering men in their morning suits—not to mention the perspiring bride in her duchesse satin gown. But this being England, you have to cater for all eventualities. The weather becomes a major preoccupation; you pray for a sunny day. Come a cold, wet wedding morn and some brides are not only disappointed but see it as a bad omen.

Then there's availability. You may not be able to get first choice of date *or* time at your church or reception venue (though a day other than Saturday will be less in demand). Florists and caterers may be overstretched and unable to give such good service; guests will have prior engagements or holidays booked. Summer weddings are often stacked, with several services on the same day, and you may have to bow to others' choice of floral decorations.

LEFT
A winter wedding can be beautifully romantic, particularly if you are fortunate with the weather. There are also a number of practical advantages.

Now consider the pros of a late-autumn, winter or early-spring wedding. The weather is bound to be awful, so you can stop worrying about it. You will probably get your first choice of time and date at church and reception. Most of your guests will be able to attend. It adds a highlight to an otherwise gloomy time of year. And honeymoon hotel breaks may well be cheaper.

TIMING IT RIGHT

Saturday remains far and away the most popular and convenient day. Sunday is generally not viable as few ministers look happily on the prospect, and register offices are shut. Weekdays pose problems, such as traffic in towns and guests getting time off work, leading the event to take on a hustled or business-like air. Nevertheless, many London weddings are held on Friday or other weekday evenings. The royal family marry on a Wednesday.

Apart from allowing enough time for you to prepare and for guests to get to the wedding, the time of day is governed largely by your reception—do you plan lunch, canapés, tea or dinner? Will you have an evening party as well? In any event, church weddings must take place between 8 am and 6 pm.

Areas of Responsibility

Etiquette lays down her strict brief as to who does what, but you don't have to adhere to it rigidly. Have a general campaign mapped out with areas of responsibility to prevent the two sides from jostling and to avoid exhausting thrash-it-out committee decisions. See the Checklist on pages 136–141 for a more detailed breakdown of all that has to be done. The attendants' duties are listed on pages 20–21.

THE BRIDE'S MOTHER

How much Mother throws herself into the melee depends largely on whether this is her first daughter to marry; the enthusiasm undoubtedly tends to wear off. Nevertheless, she is an important figure in the organisation. Traditionally, her particular areas of responsibility are: compiling guest list and keeping it up to date; sending out invitations; arrangements for wedding and reception, particularly venue, catering, cake and flowers; helping organise bride's and attendants' outfits; displaying wedding presents on the day.

THE BRIDE AND GROOM

The bride and groom are jointly responsible for: choosing the wedding date and type of ceremony and reception (the bride has the ultimate say, but most couples see this as a joint decision); speaking to or visiting the minister or registrar, and booking the place of marriage; visiting subsequently to discuss religious aspects, the order of service, music; putting any legal requirements into motion; arranging any special music for the ceremony; planning the wedding present list; writing thank-you letters for wedding presents; making any general legal arrangements (such as changing passports, making a Will).

THE BRIDE

The bride looks after the following areas herself: choosing the chief bridesmaid and having the final say about other attendants; choosing, usually with her mother, the dress, headdress and bouquet, going-away outfit and trousseau; choosing the attendants' outfits in consultation with grown-up bridesmaid(s) and/or children's mothers.

THE GROOM

The groom is individually responsible for: choosing the best man and having the final say over ushers; choosing his wedding and going-away attire; arranging transport to the wedding and for going away; arranging honeymoon; buying presents for best man and attendants; giving a speech at the wedding.

LEFT

For your wedding day to run as smoothly as possible, delegating responsibilities early on in the proceedings is essential. The first hurdle is to decide exactly what you want, then you can agree how to share the workload.

WHO PAYS FOR WHAT

No one should feel embarrassed about offering to lend a financial hand, although some parents of the bride are determined to do it all themselves. It is more and more common for the bride and groom themselves to pay for parts of the wedding, particularly if they want their own way, and also if they are living together. Alternatively, they may take on the major part of the organisation, while parents sign the cheques. Here is the traditional form.

Bride's side: newspaper announcements (though the groom may pay for this); invitations (in practice, the groom's side will probably send invitations to their guests); cake; everything for the reception (in practice, the groom's side often pays for drink or helps pay for another part of the reception); floral decorations; bride's and attendants' outfits (though attendants' parents often help out); bride's trousseau; all hire cars that involve the bride, though the groom may pay for the going-away transport as part of the honeymoon; photographer; video; wedding ring and present for the groom.

Groom's side: engagement and wedding rings; possibly the newspaper announcements; his outfit; church or register office fees; certificates and licences; his car to church and possibly the going-away transport; bouquets, headdresses and buttonholes; presents for the attendants; present for the bride; (optional) help with reception costs; honeymoon.

Planning the Ceremony

THE MARRIAGE CEREMONY IS THE FOCUS OF YOUR WEDDING DAY. THOSE FEW

MINUTES WHEN YOU SAY THE VOWS ARE PERHAPS THE MOST SIGNIFICANT PART

OF THE WHOLE DAY. CAREFUL THOUGHT MUST GO INTO CHOOSING THE PLACE

OF MARRIAGE, PLANNING THE SERVICE, DECIDING ON THE MUSIC, AND

SELECTING YOUR SUPPORTERS—THE BEST MAN, USHERS, CHIEF BRIDESMAID

AND HER COHORTS. AS LONG AS THE CEREMONY PROCEEDS ACCORDING TO

PLAN, YOU WILL BE ABLE TO RELAX AND RELISH THE CELEBRATIONS.

Booking the Church or Register Office

Planning the marriage ceremony requires serious thought and preparation. Although there are moves afoot to register buildings such as hotels and stately homes for marriage, at present the basic choice is between a registered place of worship and a register office. Most couples who have not been married before choose the full religious service (as long as there is no legal or religious impediment). Nevertheless, about one-fifth of first marriages in England and Wales take place in a register office. A swifter and simpler ceremony than a religious service, it may be the only way—or a more appropriate one—for you, and will probably prove more economical.

There are several alternative sets of requirements for both church and register-office marriages.

CHURCH OF ENGLAND

Banns: This is the most traditional mode of marriage, for which you must marry in the parish in which either you, your fiancé, or one set of parents, resides. Customarily, it is the parish of the parental home of the bride. Provided the church is not booked up, and your minister is in agreement, this takes a minimum of about a month. The banns announce your intended marriage. If the groom and bride have different parish churches, the banns must be called in both and a certificate of proof is required from the church where the wedding will not take place. On three Sundays prior to marriage, the names of both partners are read out (you don't have to disclose all your Christian names) and the public are given the opportunity to declare any just cause or impediment to the union—a chance for some unknown spouse to rear their head. Folklore decrees, in its macabre fashion, that no bride should hear her banns being called lest her children be born deaf and dumb. It is bad luck for the banns to be called partly in one year and partly in the next or even 'straddling the quarters'. The most favourable time for them to be called is between a new and full moon.

Common Licence: The only requirement to marry by this method is that one of the couple should be resident in the parish for 15 days before applying for the licence via their minister. The scheme adopted by some couples of leaving a pair of shoes in a suitcase at an address in the parish as 'proof of residency' is not looked upon kindly by the Church.

Special Licence: A discretionary licence granted by the Archbishop of Canterbury, this document makes allowances as to the time and place of the wedding. It is normally applied for by couples who wish to marry outside their own parishes (perhaps in a church with sentimental or professional connections, such as a school, college or military chapel—there needs to be a good reason, not just a whim). As a courtesy, you should discuss your intentions with your own parish minister as well as with the minister of the chosen church. It is also possible to marry in the Church of England after obtaining a superintendent registrar's certificate; for more details about this, see pages 30–31.

A minister from outside your parish: You may wish to involve a clergyman from outside your parish—an old friend, for example. He may officiate instead of your parish priest; or he may participate in addition, by reading the address or

ABOVE
The most traditional form of marriage in this country takes place in a Church of England ceremony in the parish church of the bride's parental home.

ABOVE

In a small church or chapel, where space is limited, you may have to ask only close friends and family to the service itself, and invite other friends to the reception. Seating in the church must be carefully planned.

some prayers. (If the parish priest is present, only he can hear the vows.) Taking care not to offend anyone, you will need to discuss your wishes with both parties.

Cathedral weddings: Unless the cathedral is also your parish church, you will need a special connection with the cathedral if you want to hold the wedding there. Discuss the matter with the dean.

Which service? Both the original marriage service of 1662 and the revised version of 1928 appear in the 1928 Book of Common Prayer. They are the most commonly used, and are very similar, but the revised version omits the bride's vow of obedience. 'To love, cherish and to obey' was a vow the Duchess of York took, but the Princess of Wales forsook. The 1980 Alternative Service Book uses less poetic language—'I give you this ring as a sign of our marriage' rather than 'With this ring I thee wed'; you promise to 'love' and 'cherish', with an optional 'worship', but there is no obedience required. In the United States they say 'I do', but in all versions of the marriage service in

Britain the response is 'I will'. For more information, contact the Enquiry Centre, Church House, Great Smith Street, London SW1, tel. (071) 222 9011.

OTHER DENOMINATIONS

All non-Anglican marriages require a superintendent registrar's certificate or certificate with licence (see pages 30–31). The church must be registered, and your minister authorised to register marriages. If he is not, a registrar will have to be present at the service.

Roman Catholic: The first step is to talk to your parish priest, who is responsible for all documentation regarding the church regulations. In any special circumstances, such as marrying outside your parish, he will know exactly what to do, fill in any forms and gain any necessary dispensations or letters of freedom. He will also advise you whether you need a registrar at the service. He will want to talk about the purpose and commitment of marriage, about children, and so on; you will be expected to attend at least four instructions. Decide whether you want a Nuptial Mass, during which you receive Holy Communion, or a simpler ceremony. It is usual to have special readings and prayers in addition to the basic service. For more information, contact the Catholic Marriage Advisory Council, Clitherow House, 1 Blythe Mews, Blythe Road, London W14, tel. (071) 371 1341.

Jewish: This is the only non-Christian marriage ceremony that is both civil and religious. It can take place any time (except the Sabbath) and any place (usually a synagogue), as long as it is held under a chuppah or wedding canopy. When you have obtained a superintendent registrar's certificate, you must then apply for authorisation from the Chief Rabbi, allowing three weeks. The bride and groom need one witness each, preferably a parent, plus a number of documents; ask your rabbi for fuller details. More information about Jewish weddings can be obtained from the Jewish Marriage Council, 23 Ravenshurst Avenue, London NW4, tel. (081) 203 6311.

Other non-Christian religions: All other non-Christians are required to marry in a register office. After that, they may have a religious service in their own place of worship.

Scotland: In Scotland, you don't need parental consent to marry between the ages of 16 and 18. (Young lovers still flock to Gretna Green—first stop over the border—to tie the knot.) Neither do you need to marry in your parish church—you have the freedom of the land, and that includes a house, a hotel, even a Highland hillock. For both religious and civil ceremonies, you must give notice to the registrar of the district where you want to marry, allowing 15 days. He will supply you with the necessary marriage schedule, after which you must marry within three months.

MARRIAGES OF MIXED RELIGION

Protestant churches are quite happy about marriage among their different denominations. The procedure between Catholics and baptised non-Catholics is more complicated. Catholics need 'express permission' to marry out of their faith, and promise not to defect from the faith and to baptise and bring up children in the Catholic Church. The non-Catholic is expected only to attend the standard Catholic instructions on the meaning of marriage. The marriage normally takes place in the Catholic Church, often without the Nuptial Mass. It may take place in a Protestant church, with special dispensation from the bishop. A booklet on mixed marriages is published by the Catholic Marriage Advisory Council.

Marriage between a Christian and non-Christian in a place of worship is no light matter. It would be wrong for a non-Christian to marry in church if he did not believe in the Christian doctrine, and the Church would be unlikely to sanction it. The Jewish faith does not accept a mixed marriage in a synagogue; the ceremony must be held in a register office.

MEETING THE MINISTER OR REGISTRAR

Whichever type of ceremony you choose, booking should be top on your list of priorities: the more notice you can give, the better. Make an appointment with your minister or registrar, agree upon a date and time with him, and book it. In the case of religious ceremonies, you will be expected to see your minister again after the initial meeting, to discuss Christianity and marriage, children, the meaning of the vows—and the more pressing concerns of music and the service. Most couples choose music and hymns and then go through the order of service, the address and any other additions with their minister. The Anglican marriage service does not include lessons or readings, but these can be added with the agreement of your minister.

SERVICE SHEET

The service sheet is normally used in conjunction with prayer books and so there is no need to print out the marriage service itself or the prayers, except where there is a response from the congregation. It is normally a folded sheet of fine card (fine so that it can be folded again and put in a tailcoat pocket or handbag), and it should not be engraved—it is not a formal or social item but a functional item simply to inform and assist guests. On the cover it states the name and location of the church, the date, and the initials or Christian name of the bride (on the bottom left) and groom (bottom right). When giving the order to the printer, you will need to state the hymn or psalm number, the first line, the number of verses required and which version. The sheets need not be ordered at the same time as the invitations—a few weeks before the wedding should provide ample time.

PRACTICALITIES

Your minister could be a useful ally in the organisation of aspects of the wedding. For example, he can put you in touch with the church flower-arranging team. (With regard to this, find out whether your chosen date is

LEFT
*Signing on the dotted
line . . . After the prayers and
blessing, the newlyweds, their
attendants and their parents
crowd into the vestry, sighing
with relief and brimming
with chatter about the
ceremony and guests.*

affected by the ecclesiastical calendar—some churches don't like flowers during Lent, for example.) Check the parking arrangements—particularly if your wedding date is a busy one. Take a notebook for suggestions and an existing service sheet as a guide for working out your order of service.

You should also discuss fees, which, on top of the marriage service and certificate, could include the banns or licence, organist, choir, bell ringers, heating, flowers, photographs, video, clearing up confetti, etc. These fees should be paid promptly just before or after the wedding, direct to each person involved, by the best man on behalf of the groom.

While you are at the church, decide exactly how many guests you can fit in, and make sure there is enough room on each pew. Don't try to squeeze eight on to a pew that is designed for six. Work out a seating plan for close relations in the first two or three pews on each side.

THE REHEARSAL

Arrange for a rehearsal in the week before the wedding. Those attending should be the bride, groom, best man, bride's father or whoever is giving the bride away, matron of honour/bridesmaids, pages, and ushers (and mothers or nannies of little children). If you do have small children in attendance, take a sheet to pin on your dress so they get used to a long dress or train. Send the children home once they have rehearsed their part to prevent them from getting overtired and over-excited. Find out where the lavatory is. Brief the ushers about seating, and give them your seating plan. Appoint one or two ushers to escort the bride's mother, groom's parents, etc, to their seats.

REGISTER OFFICE WEDDING

There are many reasons for a register office wedding, such as remarriage, the marriage of partners of different faiths, or just the desire for a simple wedding.

RIGHT

A register office wedding. If the room has all the reverential overtones of a parlour, this is the aim—the civil ceremony makes a conscious effort to avoid any religious connotations.

The superintendent registrar will be able to advise you about the service, how many guests may be invited (a minimum of two, to witness the signing of the register, and a maximum of about 20 or 30), and whether you may have flowers, photographs, video and music. Note that any music must be secular as this is not a religious service. Book early—register offices are particularly busy on Saturday mornings (most are shut in the afternoon).

Superintendent registrar's certificate: This is not the marriage certificate, but one issued to allow you to marry. Both parties must have resided in a registration district for at least seven days (though not necessarily the same district). On day eight, each must go to his or her respective register office and give notice of intention to marry, specifying the building in which the marriage is to take place, giving other details and signing the official declaration. Evidence of

birth if under 23, certified evidence of the death of a former spouse or dissolution of marriage if applicable, and a passport or other form of identity if foreign are all required. The marriage then takes place between 22 days and three months later.

Certificate with licence: One party must have resided in the registration district for 15 days (the other need not be resident in the country). On day 16, both parties must be in the country, when they give notice to the registrar. After one clear working day, they will be issued a certificate and licence, after which marriage may take place. For more information, contact the General Register Office, St Catherine's House, 10 Kingsway, London WC2, tel. (071) 242 0262. Or contact your local Superintendent Registrar.

REMARRIAGE

It is against Church of England rulings for a divorcee to remarry in church while the spouse is still living, but a minister may agree to officiate at his discretion. The Catholic Church takes a strict view, but Nonconformists allow remarriages in church. However, the usual course would be to marry in a register office, perhaps followed by a service of blessing. Widowed persons are free to remarry as they wish, in a standard religious or civil ceremony.

SERVICE OF BLESSING

A church service of blessing (properly called a Service of Prayer and Dedication) may be held after a civil ceremony. It can be held in any church, not necessarily in your parish, directly after the marriage or on another day. The service includes hymns, prayers, readings, an address and the blessing, but no vows. Discuss it with your minister and book a date in the usual way.

Church Music

The church music is an intrinsic and important part of the marriage ceremony. It sets and echoes the mood of the service. There is the subdued, anticipatory music while the congregation awaits the bride, breaking into a rousing tune at her entrance, then continuing with hymns, psalms and anthems until the jubilant, climactic chords to announce the departure of the wedded couple.

This is a chance for you and the groom to stamp your own personality on your marriage service, in consultation with the minister and church organist. Your first step is to discover, discreetly, the virtuosity of the regular organist and—if there is one—the choir. Most couples are happy with the resident team. However, if it doesn't match up to your musical aspirations, you may wish to draft in your own musicians. They could include singers and/or instrumentalists drawn from family, friends, a local society or a school choir. An outside choir may wish to provide their own organist. Meanwhile, you must check whether there are choir stalls and how many people can be accommodated.

Once you have enlisted your musicians, you are free to choose what they play—within bounds. Bear in mind suitability of tempo, mood and words. Anything quirky is dreaded by most church organists. There are standard

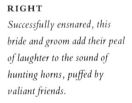

RIGHT

Successfully ensnared, this bride and groom add their peal of laughter to the sound of hunting horns, puffed by valiant friends.

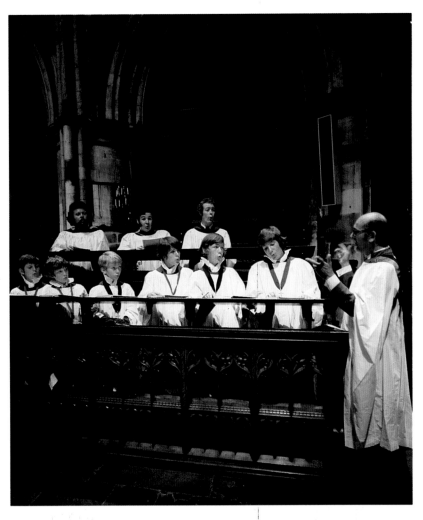

LEFT
Many couples arrange for a choir to sing during their wedding. The choir may be affiliated to the church or it may come from outside, perhaps from another church or from a local school.

pieces, hackneyed pieces and frankly unsuitable pieces. Bach, Handel and Purcell are the most popular. Wagner's and Mendelssohn's Wedding Marches are the most clichéd entrance and departure tunes; Wagner's ('Here comes the bride...') is rarely played these days, but Mendelssohn's gets an occasional airing. Unsuitable for the most part, though oft-requested, are pop songs (*Sailing*, *A Whiter Shade of Pale*), soundtracks from films and stage musicals, and all things dirge-like and funereal.

PRE-SERVICE AND PROCESSIONAL MUSIC

The music leading up to the service should set the tone for the ceremony—you can't go wrong with Bach and the Baroque. The processional music, chosen by the bride, is dignified and stirring. A trumpet's resonant tones will herald your entrance beautifully, or you could, like the Queen, walk up the aisle to a hymn. Choose something with a steady pace that can be broken at a suitable moment when you reach the chancel steps. Time the music against the walk up the aisle—the two must end in unison or all impact will be lost.

Favourite notes to enter on include Clarke's *Trumpet Voluntary*, Purcell's *Trumpet Tune and Air*, the Grand March from Verdi's *Aïda*, Bach's *Fugue in G*

Minor, Handel's *Water Music* and *Arrival of the Queen of Sheba*, the Wedding March from Mozart's *The Marriage of Figaro* and, to a lesser extent these days, the Wedding March from Wagner's *Lohengrin*.

HYMNS AND PSALMS

The standard order of service is hymn, psalm, hymn, but many couples prefer to have three hymns. It is best to choose hymns the majority of your guests will recognise, though if yours is the fifteenth 'Praise my soul' or 'Praise to the Lord' that season, it could be reduced to a meaningless chant. A choir to lead hymns and sing descants makes a world of difference. Go through the hymns with the organist beforehand to make sure he or she will play the right version, at the right tempo, in an acceptable key. (Where wording varies, make sure also that you mark the right version for the printer of the service sheet.) It is worth checking verses for unsuitable words. You can always cut an offending verse, but ask your minister's advice.

Top hymns include *Praise, my soul, the King of heaven*; *Praise to the Lord, the Almighty*; *Guide me, O thou great Redeemer*; *The Lord's my Shepherd* (Psalm 23), to the tune of Crimond; *Dear Lord and Father of mankind*; *Immortal, invisible*; *I vow to thee my country*; *Jerusalem*; *Lead us, heavenly Father, lead us*; *Love divine, all loves excelling*; *Come down, O love divine*; *The King of love, my shepherd is*; *Glorious things of thee are spoken*; *Lord of all hopefulness*.

Favourite psalms are Nos 23 (various choral arrangements if not sung as a hymn), 121, 128, 37 and 48.

DURING THE SIGNING OF THE REGISTER

The ten-minute gap while you are in the vestry is the ideal time for instrumentalists to play, for the choir to sing an anthem, or for the organist to have free rein (*Jesu joy of man's desiring* is a favourite). A soloist can be very moving, but do ask a professional.

RECESSIONAL MUSIC

The triumphant procession down the aisle should be carried off with true pomp and circumstance. Widor's *Toccata* is one of the most demanded and demanding pieces to stride out to: Other suggested notes to go out on are Clarke's *Trumpet Voluntary*; Mendelssohn's Wedding March from *A Midsummer Night's Dream*; Bach's *Ave Maria*; Handel's *Music for the Royal Fireworks*; and Pachelbel's *Toccata in C*.

BELL APPEAL

One of the most glorious sounds is that of church bells announcing your wedding day to the neighbourhood, and a further outbreak ringing the changes as you emerge from church. Arranging bell-ringers should pose no particular problem; your minister will know whom to call upon if there are no regular bell-ringers at your church.

RIGHT
The music you choose to accompany you back down the aisle traditionally has an air of triumph and glory, adding to the buoyant mood of everyone concerned.

The Attendants

ABOVE

Young attendants are largely decorative appendages to the bridal entourage, giving scope for adding splashes of colour— particularly in the form of random flowers—to a predominantly white theme.

The wedding entourage would not be complete without attendants. Do not underestimate their value. Not just a row of pretty/handsome faces, they have important roles to play leading up to and during the wedding day. The chief bridesmaid is assistant, supporter, morale-booster and confidante to the bride. The best man's job is even more demanding—as well as all the above, he is peace-keeper, liaison officer, minder, guardian angel, public speaker and wit.

THE BRIDE'S ATTENDANTS

It is completely up to you whether you have just one grown-up bridesmaid or matron of honour (the title for a bridesmaid who is married and who usually acts as chief bridesmaid), a herd of tiny maids, or a pride of pageboys. One survey shows that three bridesmaids and one pageboy are the average; another finds two to three maids are quite the thing, but decidedly *no* pages. The number of attendants depends on two main factors: budget and protocol.

Traditionally, the bride invites first her own sisters, then the groom's sisters, and finally her friends or more distant relations to be bridesmaids. The chief bridesmaid is usually the bride's sister or best friend. If you have several equally close friends, it may be wise to avoid offence being taken by having only young attendants. Although toddlers look sweet and adorable, they *can* spoil things—the service, the photographs, their outfits. Do think carefully about inviting very young ones to accompany you up the aisle.

When you have made your choice, check first that the parents are keen, then write to each attendant individually, on a fun card in the case of children.

It is customary to give attendants and the best man a token present on the day, such as a piece of jewellery, a decorative box, an inscribed book, a pen, or some other lasting souvenir of the day. The bride may choose the gifts, but it is the groom who pays for them.

DUTIES OF THE CHIEF BRIDESMAID

- Helping the bride choose her wedding outfit and trousseau
- Organising the hen night in conjunction with the bride, arranging the venue and any props or surprises
- Going to rehearsal
- Possibly staying the night before the wedding at the bride's home; in the morning, helping the bride (and perhaps young attendants) to dress and generally giving support and encouragement
- Arriving at church about ten minutes before the service

RIGHT

Candy stripes and lace for a young bridesmaid and page. A certain amount of tact may have to be shown when selecting young attendants from a large pool of brothers, sisters, nieces, nephews, cousins and godchildren.

RIGHT

*Grown-up bridesmaids—
usually sisters or close friends
of the bride—play a
supporting role to the chief
bridesmaid. Here, wearing
simple white with yellow
detailing, they are followed by
pageboys dressed as mascots of
the Household Cavalry.*

- Checking other attendants' clothes, headdresses and bouquets; and assembling the attendants ready to enter church (it's best if she brings up the rear, to keep an eye on the children)
- When the bride arrives at church, arranging her veil and train
- Stepping forward to take the bride's bouquet when they reach the chancel steps, and returning it to her after the signing of the register, for the triumphal march down the aisle
- Helping to round up and organise younger attendants for the photographs
- At the reception being always on hand to tend to the bride and, like the best man, being on standby for family duties, such as looking after little bridesmaids and pages
- Helping the bride change out of her wedding dress; possibly taking charge of it (but usually the bride's mother does this)

THE BRIDE'S OTHER ATTENDANTS

The bride's other attendants have no responsibilities other than to be present and correct and do as they are asked by the chief bridesmaid. Older ones may be called upon to help in general duties and introducing themselves to guests. Youngsters are simply required not to tread on the bride's train/ scream/yawn/run off throughout the service.

THE GROOM'S ATTENDANTS

The groom is backed up by his best man and ushers. Although the ushers may be drawn from the bride's side too, the best man is traditionally a brother or best friend of the groom. There is no set number of ushers—you can have anything from two or three to six or more, depending on the size of the church

and the number of candidates. You need one head usher and at least one who knows the other side of the family. The groom's side is usually more heavily represented than the bride's, as this is a diplomatic way of giving his *other* best friends a role in the wedding. The groom may like to write to his best man, but there is no need to invite ushers formally.

DUTIES OF THE BEST MAN
- Helping to choose/hire the groom's wedding outfit
- Organising and attending the stag night with the groom, and ushering him safely home
- Helping to organise transport to the ceremony, reception and the first stage of the honeymoon
- Attending the rehearsal
- Conferring with the groom and his family over who takes responsibility for the following: service sheets, buttonholes, the groom's going-away outfit, honeymoon suitcase and travel documents, the going-away car; possibly

ABOVE

The perfect solution for keeping your herd of tiny tots in order. Each bridesmaid and page is attached by floral swags to another, in order of age and responsibility, so that none may go astray.

*Baby English roses: in pink
and white, with rose-laden
haloes and baskets of blossoms,
these two young bridesmaids
are on their best behaviour
for the big day.*

having to make sure some or all of these things are in the right place for the
wedding day

- Helping the groom get ready and getting him to the church/register office
  on time (a good 20 minutes before the service)
- Making sure all fees are paid to the minister or registrar, organist, bell-
  ringers and any other musicians
- Keeping the wedding ring(s) safe until needed in the service
- Escorting the chief bridesmaid to the vestry and down the aisle
- Helping to round up family for the photographs and organise lifts to the
  reception and parking; accompanying the bridesmaids to the reception (he is
  the last of the bridal party to leave the church)
- Possibly helping in general family duties at the reception and speeding guests
  along the receiving line
- Organising the timing of the speeches and cake cutting if there is no master
  of ceremonies, and announcing their onset to the guests; giving the third and

LEFT
Sebastian Conran is handsomely attended by his fashionable friends, each sporting a dark morning suit and flamboyant buttonhole. The groom's attendants are by no means just peacocks on parade, however—the best man's job is perhaps the most demanding of all.

final speech and thanking the groom for his toast to the bridesmaids on their behalf; reading out any telemessages
- Making sure the couple get changed on time, announcing their impending departure, and making sure everyone is gathered round outside to bid the couple farewell
- Possibly making a few decorative additions to the going-away transport, which is entrusted to his care, but preventing any damage being done
- After the departure of the bride and groom, being on hand to help out in general; possibly taking charge of the groom's wedding clothes

DUTIES OF THE USHERS

- Attending the rehearsal, where they are briefed about seating in church
- Arriving at the church 30 to 40 minutes before the service
- Taking umbrellas if raining, to escort guests into church and to protect the bridal party afterwards
- Handing out service sheets and directing guests to their seats (bride's side on the left, groom's on the right)
- Escorting the bride's mother and the groom's parents to their seats (it is nice to escort grandparents personally as well)
- Making sure the rest of the immediate family is seated in the front pews or according to the seating plan
- Sitting down as soon as the bride's mother is seated
- At least one usher sitting at the back to seat latecomers
- After the service, helping the best man in his general duties, such as gathering guests for photographs and arranging transport

A Sense of Occasion

FROM YOUR GUESTS' FIRST SIGHT OF YOUR WEDDING INVITATIONS TO THEIR

LAST GLIMPSE OF YOU AS YOU LEAVE THE RECEPTION, YOUR WEDDING WILL

HAVE A UNIQUE AND SPECIAL ATMOSPHERE. FLOWERS ARE A KEY FACTOR, AND

THE FORM OF TRANSPORT YOU CHOOSE CAN ALSO ADD GREATLY TO THE SENSE

OF OCCASION. CAREFUL PLANNING OF ALL THESE ELEMENTS IS ESSENTIAL—

RIGHT DOWN TO THE PHOTOGRAPHER/VIDEO-MAKER, WHO IDEALLY WILL

CAPTURE THE ATMOSPHERE OF YOUR WEDDING ON FILM.

The Guest List and Invitations

Discuss guests with your parents, your fiancé and his parents. To determine numbers, each side should make out a rough list, taking into account the number you can fit into the church and reception, and your budget. The allocation will normally be divided equally between bride's and groom's sides, but there are obvious exceptions according to the size and whereabouts of each side's family.

As a matter of courtesy, invitations should be sent to the minister, the groom's family, the best man and grown-up attendants (children are included on their parents' invitation), and any friends and relations who you know will not be able to attend the wedding.

Both sides should compile a final guest list and the groom's list should be sent to the bride's mother. Either side may send out the groom's invitations, but replies normally go to the bride's mother. However, if you are the host, or are taking care of the organisation, you could make the RSVP address your own or that of your fiancé.

TRADITIONAL INVITATIONS

A wedding is a formal social function where the traditional style for invitations is laid down to the last copperplate full stop. This style is accepted as 'correct' inasmuch as anything is correct in the social language—it's like wearing a grey morning suit to Ascot. Of course, you don't *have* to adhere to social conventions, and if your wedding is at a register office or is a small or casual affair, you may feel formal invitations are inappropriate (in which case, see the advice about informal invitations on pages 46–47).

A 'proper' invitation should be hand-engraved in copperplate script: for each set of invitations, a skilled craftsman engraves an individual copper plate in mirror-writing. It has a quivery fineness that cannot be achieved by machine typesetting. The print is customarily black on single-fold double-sheet card. The traditional size is 17.5×13 cm/$7 \times 5\frac{1}{2}$ inches (Duke), but nowadays the majority of invitations are 20×15 cm/8×6 inches (Albert).

Alternative printing processes are thermography (shiny, embossed and an inexpensive emulation of engraving) and lithography (plain, flat, unpretentious, and the cheapest of all).

RIGHT
The guests at the wedding of Sebastian Conran and Georgina Godley were as much of a spectacle as the bridal entourage. Brides need not be the only people taking inspiration from period dress.

There are very few old-fashioned engravers around, but you don't need to find a local service—it can all be done by post. Ask stationers to show or send samples of their work—most have packs of sample invitations and service sheets plus an order form with suggested wording. Non-specialists are best avoided since they don't have their own engravers, take longer and cannot offer the same personal service. Printers should be able to print in Hebrew and foreign languages if given due notice. For processes other than engraving, any printer should suffice.

WORDING

The invitation shown on the right, opposite, contains the standard wording of the formal invitation. For alternative wording where the host(s) differ from the standard, consult your printer or *Debrett's Correct Form*. Wording for the service of blessing is the same as the wedding invitation, except that the invitations 'request the pleasure of your company at a Service of Blessing following the marriage of ...'. A reception-only invitation can either follow the wedding invitation format (... 'request the pleasure of your company at a reception following the marriage of Mary to Mr Joseph Alexander Jones, at the Royal Hotel, Alton, on ...'), or take the form of an 'At home' card. For an additional evening party, enclose a separate 'At home' invitation.

You should never state the form of dress on the invitation. If you would like men to wear morning suits (or indeed, if you have any other special wishes), make it known through word of mouth. Do make it clear if children are not welcome in church and if there is to be a creche—enclose a note with the invitations, or let guests know by telephone nearer the date.

In the case of cancellation or postponement, a printed card is sent to guests, with wording along the following lines: 'Owing to the recent death (illness) of Mr Edward Miller, Mr and Mrs John Miller deeply regret that they are obliged to cancel (postpone) the invitations to the marriage of their daughter Mary to Mr Joseph Jones on Saturday, 6th July, 1991. (...their daughter Mary to Mr Joseph Jones at St Mark's Church, Alton, from Saturday, 6th July, 1991, to Saturday, 10th August, 1991.)'

INFORMAL INVITATIONS

Individualists and the budget-bound could design their own invitations, ask an artist friend, or work with a stationer to dream up an individual design. Novel invitations have included a comic strip using the bride and groom as models, cards made around a transparent envelope full of confetti, and printed balloons. Possibly the ultimate was a folder of no less than seven invitations per guest, edged and printed in 22-carat gold.

Understated but stylish invitations could be written by a calligrapher or could incorporate a monogram or hand-engraving of your house. Coloured or textured paper, unorthodox lettering, borders, ribbons, unusual-shaped cards, all contribute a personal stamp—but avoid gilding the lily. It is much better

Christopher Bown and Lorna Parker

request the pleasure of

your company at their marriage

at Queens' College Chapel, Cambridge

on Saturday, 17th October 1987

at 3 o'clock

and afterwards in the

Old Combination Room

R.S.V.P.
1 Bridstow Place
London W2

Colonel Sir Henry and Lady Tremayne
request the pleasure of
your company at the marriage
of their daughter
Annabelle
to
Captain James Paul Parker-Allen
at St. Luke's, Stamfordham
on Saturday, 12th September, 1987
at 3 o'clock
and afterwards at
Wootton Old Hall.

R. S. V. P.
Wootton Old Hall,
Stamfordham,
Northumberland.

ABOVE

A slightly less formal invitation than the one on the right. Note the bride and groom are host and hostess. This is the only social invitation where the host and hostess invite the guests, rather than just the hostess.

ABOVE

Traditional wording in copperplate script. Whether your parents request the pleasure or the honour of their guests' company, and whether your marriage will be to or with your fiancé is up to you.

either to stick to tradition or go all-out for something wacky than to treat your guests to an overdose of schmaltz.

Once you dispense with conventional presentation, you can word the invitation any way you want.

SENDING OUT INVITATIONS

Invitations should be ordered at least three months before the day, to leave a comfortable margin, and sent out about six weeks in advance (eight in high season, if you want your wedding to gain precedence over the many others jostling to be attended).

Remember only one invitation is needed per married couple; children below the age of majority should be included on the same invitation. Children over 18 (or 21) should get their own invitation. The names of the guest(s) should be handwritten in ink (not ballpoint pen) in the top left-hand corner, yet the envelope should be addressed to Mrs William Guest only. *Debrett's Correct Form* should enlighten you over titles and ranks; do note any variation between address on the invitation and on the envelope. Mrs William Guest addresses her reply and the envelope to Mrs James Hostess alone.

People are so lax about replying promptly (it is good manners to reply immediately) that more and more invitations state RSVP by a certain date; some hostesses resort to enclosing a stamped addressed reply card.

Wedding Presents

Just as you begin to feel exhausted with the whole wedding business, things start to look up. At last! The material reward for all your efforts—a healthy heap of presents. Even though you may know what is in each package, nothing quite beats the thrill of tearing off the silvery ribbons-and-bells wrapping paper, rustling through the tissue, and inspecting what's inside.

THE WEDDING LIST

If you are to avoid the Ten Toast-Racks Syndrome, it is worth having a wedding list. Some couples feel it is mercenary and unspontaneous to state in precise detail what they want, but special friends who have their own ideas can always deviate from the list, while others who are lacking inspiration will value guidance. It also helps guests who live abroad or far away, as they can order by telephone, and it cuts down on monstrosities as well as duplications.

Major department stores offer a wedding list service. Eight to ten weeks before the wedding, you and your fiancé visit each floor making a note of all you want; some stores have suggestion lists for you to tick. The store then types out your personal list and takes care of all purchases and deliveries, striking out each item as it is bought. Arrange your list at one or two stores.

Bear these questions in mind: how quickly can they produce the list? (It varies from a couple of days to a week.) Do they give you a duplicate list? Do they gift-wrap and do they charge for the service? Do they provide gift cards? Do they keep you constantly informed so that you know what to strike off the list and can start writing the thank-you letters? Do they deliver free of charge? How often do they deliver to your area? If an item goes out of stock, how long will it take for the new order to arrive? Some stores offer extra services—at Harrods, where the list is computerised, customers can request a print-out of presents in their price-range.

Alternatively, you could make out your own list, specifying the model and colour of each item, and photocopy it for family and friends. Put your mother in charge of keeping the list up-to-date, and ask everyone to check with her before they buy and inform her of any purchases.

THANK-YOU LETTERS

Everyone invited should send a present, whether they are able to attend the wedding or not. From the first flurry of deliveries soon after people receive their invitations, until the day and beyond, presents will keep arriving. Don't let 200 thank-you letters mount up. Keep a record of all presents and their donors, and make a point of writing the letters straightaway.

Transport

Y ou will need a chauffeur-driven vehicle—even if the 'chauffeur' is a friend—to take you and your father to church, and the same vehicle to take you and the groom from church to the reception. You may also need a car for your attendants. The groom may want to borrow a car or use his own or the best man's, but should not try to drive himself to church; often the best man acts as chauffeur.

A LIMOUSINE OR VINTAGE CAR

The classic, monster black wedding limousine is a Dorchester. The other, more widely available limo is the Daimler. Both are smart, smooth, purring motors with lots of leg (train) room and head (veil) room. A more flamboyant option is a white Rolls-Royce.

A vintage car looks pretty, and it's fun to wave from an open-top Twenties Phantom. But you have to proceed at a snail's pace because there is little protection from the wind. On the way to the church, for the sake of decorum and staying unruffled, it is wise to have the hood up. Remember too that these cars are delicate creatures, only able to cover short distances, and not keen on standing around in hot weather. One hire company admits that their elderly cars sometimes need a push start, but they find 'it adds to the fun'. Book early as there are not many classic cars around. Look at the car before you book,

ABOVE

Looking every bit the Pre-Raphaelite tragi-heroine, Victoria Lockwood steps down from her coach-and-horses, bound for the church where she will become Viscountess Althorp.

and make sure this is definitely the one you'll be getting on the day. It is unwise to use a vintage car to go away in. You don't need ribbons on an antique car— it's a case of lily-gilding.

A HORSE AND CARRIAGE

This is another romantic option to take you from church to reception, but it can only be used for short distances, which is probably a good thing as it's not too comfortable, spacious or easy to get in and out of. The most common choice is a Brougham, single or double—most go for the four-seater Double Brougham. A Landau is good in winter as it can be open or completely closed.

When booking, do be honest about any steep hills en route. It won't necessarily mean that you can't have a horse-drawn carriage, but that they will give you a carriage with brakes and may change the horse's shoes beforehand.

FROM CHURCH TO RECEPTION

Arranging transport logistics can be a knotty brainteaser. For example, on arrival at church, Car A contains bride and father, Car B bridesmaids and pages (and possibly bride's mother), Car C (optional) more bridesmaids and pages, Car D the groom and best man. Then, on departure for the reception, Car A contains the bride and groom, Cars B and C the bridesmaids and pages and

ABOVE
Katie Rabett lets Kit Hesketh-Harvey take the reins as they head off for their honeymoon at a healthy trot.

best man, Car D has no driver, and the bride's parents have no car. Add sisters and brothers and non-driving grandmothers and uncles on both sides, and you have a sophisticated puzzle. Think through your particular case in advance, making sure that everyone knows his duties and who's collecting/giving lifts to whom, and that everyone has the necessary car keys.

GOING AWAY

After the reception, a modern chauffeur-driven car or taxi is a better idea than driving your own car. You'll avoid any witty vandalism, drunk-driving charges and other dampeners on the day, and can continue to feel relaxed and unflustered about traffic and getting somewhere in time.

Boats, hot-air balloons, and helicopters are more exciting options. If yours is a riverside reception, then be theatrical and float off across the water in a launch or even a rowing boat or a punt. As each case is so individual, you will have to arrange it locally. Balloons are dependent on fine weather, and if it's too windy they won't risk taking off—so be prepared to be disappointed.

You don't need a lycra jumpsuit to go away by helicopter, but you will have to hold on to your hat. The model most likely to whisk you away from your front lawn is the four-seater Jet Ranger. Any lawn or car park in the countryside is a perfect helipad, but helicopters have to avoid town centres.

The Photographs

ABOVE
A portrait of a young lady.
This bridesmaid has been
captured in close-up, her head
framed initially by her halo of
roses and then by a mottled
background of trees and flowers
thrown out-of-focus.

Wedding photographs have an importance all of their own. They are the one immediate visual record that everyone can have access to. A good photographer is vital, since his representation of your wedding is how it will be remembered in the future.

The wedding photographer's art is a mixture of reportage (like a newspaper photographer) and portraiture. He has to work quickly and unobtrusively, with little time to prepare lighting or backgrounds, and no room for trial and error. It is by no means easy, and there is heavy pressure on the photographer to produce good results.

CHOOSING A PHOTOGRAPHER

Personal recommendation is your best lead, or you could contact the British Institute of Professional Photography, Amwell End, Ware, Hertfordshire, tel. (0920) 464011.

Photographers note a trend away from starchy formal photos in favour of a more relaxed, informal record of the wedding day. Studios divide loosely into two camps. There are those that take straightforward shots of the couple and groups, plus a general record of the day snapped at the traditional plot points. Most do candid reportage shots as an optional extra. Then there are those who do more contrived, 'arty' photographs, such as soft-focus portraits under the weeping willow or the best man and groom exchanging the ring.

RIGHT
Nothing brings out the
amateur photographers quite
like a wedding. Though the
bane of the official
photographer's life, guests
invariably produce some of the
most successful candid shots.

RIGHT
A beautifully balanced formal
group shot at the marriage of
Princess Alexandra's son
James Ogilvy and Julia
Rawlinson. Note the
symmetrical composition,
the framing of the couple
and best man in the archway,
and the juxtaposition of
white and black.

Ask to see the photographer's portfolio, and look out for the following:

- Definition and focus—clear images, sharp edges, unless taken purposely soft-focus
- Lighting—both indoors and out; weather conditions should not affect the quality; look for colour pictures that seem to glow
- Framing—the positioning of subjects in the viewfinder
- Group shots—are they standing in a rugby-club line-up, or are they interestingly grouped? Is everyone looking at the camera? Do they look static and uneasy?
- Portraits—are face and neck blighted by shadows of the nose and chin, or eyes squinting into the sun? Or is the face evenly lit with a gentle halo of light from behind? A good photographer can use backlighting successfully.
- Candid shots—has he captured an off-guard expression, a funny moment? Or did he miss it altogether? Does he have enchanting shots of children?

Beware of studios that produce little more than snapshots. There is no point in hiring a photographer if you don't want the pictures to look special. The natural, informal approach shouldn't be carried too far—'unposed' pictures often need a little setting up, and photographers report that brides are often happier when told where to look, what to do with their hands. The results need not look contrived.

Ask around to get an idea of the going rate, but note that quality work cannot be produced at a low cost, and cheap fees will mean cheap results. The system of charging varies. Expect either a set fee for the day, including around 80 postcard-sized colour proofs (they take about 150 but do their own selection); or a set fee and 30 to 40 large album-quality prints of your own selection presented in an album; or no attendance fee but a charge per photograph ordered. Some studios may give you a greater quantity of proofs, but you will almost certainly want to get a selection enlarged and printed on good-quality paper, which will add considerably to your original estimate.

BLACK-AND-WHITE AND SEPIA PHOTOGRAPHS

Colour is used almost exclusively these days. It needs no fanfare—it has obvious appeal and appropriateness and no one would dream of not having a colour record. But having black-and-white or sepia photographs taken along with the colour is worth considering, as they can be far superior in quality and suitability. Light and contrast can be adjusted in the printing if conditions were not ideal, whereas colour shots cannot be altered once they are processed. 'Flaws' such as spots or bright red cheeks that jump out of colour snaps are flatteringly toned down in black-and-white. Even disliked physical features can be softened with clever use of light. And the pictures can seem more statuesque and important than snap-happy multi-colour reality.

Some photographers may be reluctant to undertake black-and-white as well as colour because it is too demanding, involving an extra camera and differing lighting conditions. They almost certainly won't want to chop and change, but

RIGHT

Sealed with a kiss: a classic moment for the wedding album, framed within grand portals, with the bride's dress and train arranged in a full circle at her feet.

you should be able to persuade them to do some black-and-white at your home before the wedding and at the reception. If only colour is available, you could ask a friend to do informal black-and-whites. In this event, send films to a professional photographic firm, who will print a set of contact sheets very cheaply. Then you can choose the best shots and have them printed professionally on good paper. Black-and-white looks and prints better on matt than on glossy paper, whereas colour looks richer with a gloss.

Grainy photographs taken in black-and-white or colour on fast film are a nice way of capturing mood and romance.

BOOKING THE PHOTOGRAPHER

Photographers take bookings for up to two years in advance for summer Saturdays, so make booking a photographer top of your list of priorities. Visit the studio with your mother and fiancé to establish personal contact, assess the photographer's work and make sure both he and you are aware of each other's requirements. Bear these points in mind:

Will you actually end up with the photographer you see—and not one of his minions? Are the photos you see and like by the photographer you are booking? What equipment does he use? He should have a medium-format camera that produces large negatives for the formals (the quality is far superior) and a good camera with interchangeable lenses, from wide angle to telephoto, for reportage. Does he send colour film to a professional laboratory?

Brief him thoroughly, find out how many shots he will expect to take, and discuss any extra shots you want, if you want black-and-white as well as colour, if you want to be photographed at home before the wedding, and so on. Some brides now request a photo session before the day as well. Discuss fees and the price of extra prints. Exactly what do you get for your money? Will he need an assistant? At what cost? What travel expenses will he charge for? Note that the photographer will keep the negatives of your photographs. You may wish to clarify your rights with him.

After the initial visit, make a definite booking in writing, reiterating the main points of your discussion. Ask him in turn to give you a clear quote in writing, confirming also the time and place. Nearer the event, arrange a meeting with the actual photographer assigned to your wedding. Discuss timing, and how long to allocate for portraits and group shots. (Rushed pictures will look that way.) Run through all the moments and poses to be covered. Discuss the amount of coverage he should give to each aspect. Discuss locations, in particular for the group shots. Give him a list of who should be in the group shots, and of any other people you particularly want photographed. On the day, assign the best man, an usher or a member of the family to assist him in identifying and rounding up these people.

PHOTOGRAPHIC COVERAGE

The ideal package is to have some formal shots, some candid, some colour, some black-and-white or sepia. You could have some photographs of you at

home getting ready, plus a few portraits in the garden perhaps. The alternative, unless you have two photographers, is to have guests photographed as they arrive at the church—the ideal way to capture *all* your guests on film, when they're looking at their best. You'll also want the following: the groom's and then your arrival at the church. A few in church. The jubilant procession. The couple at the church entrance. Various groups outside the church. Getting into the car. (A shiny black limousine reflecting the bride's dress can produce some stunning results.) Candid shots at the reception. Informal shots of young bridesmaids and pages. Speeches, toasts, cake cutting. Going away amid a shower of confetti; the car; boisterous guests.

In the church, the sanctity of the service should never be disturbed. For this reason, photographs in church are few and usually done with available light—flashguns are taboo. These shots are always at the discretion of the clergy; it is the photographer's job to find out what he may take. Most churches allow photographers to come forward for the signing of the register and the triumphal procession, and very occasionally the actual vows and placing of rings (taken at the altar).

ABOVE

The groom and best man shaking hands is one of the standard shots in the official photographer's repertoire.

For a register office wedding, ask the registrar about photography inside the building. You will want a few shots as you emerge, but for group shots a more photogenic setting may be in a nearby park or at the reception.

FORMAL GROUP SHOTS

The timing on the day is very delicate. As you emerge from church, the guests will be queuing up to follow you out. There's usually time for a few quick, semi-posed shots of the bride and groom before the guests start clamouring at the portals. Then you can take one of two courses: either have the photographs taken here, or go on to the reception and have them done there.

If the weather is fine, it's a good idea not to dash off to the reception. Family and friends appreciate being able to greet you immediately after the service, and you can continue your photo session outside the church. Line up for the semi-formal shots—with attendants, then with parents too, and then with more family. Some photographers find it works better to start with the full group and gradually pare it down. There is scope for happy, relaxed, candid shots as well as posed groups. The groom with best man and ushers is a traditional shot, but ask for one with you in it too—the contrast of the bride in white against the darkness of the besuited men is a striking one.

Inevitably guests will want to take their own pictures. This is the official photographer's nightmare. With distracting cries from all directions, no one ever looks at him; also, friends' photos lose him business.

If you do go on to the reception and have the formal shots taken there, be sure to get them done before the guests arrive. Everyone is still in good order at this point, whereas, if you wait till after the hand-shaking, the bridesmaids and pages will be dishevelled and covered in cake. Some photographers will have chosen a spot in the garden—and this setting is ideal. There should also be an indoor 'studio' set up in case of rain. Do check that the room is suitable. Not only should there be enough space, but the background should not interfere with the composition of the group. One couple's entire set of formal photographs came out with a white fireplace sticking out of the bride's dress. (A good photographer should not, of course, fall into this trap.) If you have planned a cooked meal, make sure the caterers have allowed enough time for the photo session—at least half an hour.

UNOFFICIAL PHOTOGRAPHY

As with other aspects of the wedding, amateur friends can be employed. Most guests take cameras as a matter of course. But even if you ask one specially to record the day, there will be an abundance of photographs of *his* friends, and a higher proportion of poor pictures. Also, you will find that he's missed out crucial moments because he was chatting. By all means use friends as back-up—some of their photographs will probably be better than the professional's, and you can use guests' snaps to make up an alternative album. But don't rely on them to cover the whole event as a professional would.

RIGHT
A regal pose on a sweeping staircase. Photographers are right to capitalise on the grandeur and formality of the occasion and wedding dress by setting up dignified shots such as this.

The Video

'It all went so quickly and I can't remember a thing!' This is the eternal cry from both bride and groom. They race around in a euphoric cloud, talking to everyone yet hardly aware of what's being said since they are simultaneously experiencing several conversations and scanning the entire gathering. By the next morning it's all a haze and their one wish is for an action replay.

Enter the video: an hour-and-a-half to two-hour programme all about the happy couple and the big day. Before the event, some couples—particularly the groom—argue against it. 'We're not performing seals, the equipment will get in the way, we'll feel self-conscious and fluff our lines. . . .' But a professional video-maker should not provoke any uneasiness. He will stay in the background as much as possible, working with natural light. He won't ask anyone to perform for the camera; he simply records the events of the day.

BOOKING THE VIDEO-MAKER

It's essential to find the right person, as there are some who set up with cheap equipment and do the job badly. Word-of-mouth recommendation is as important as ever. It is vital to meet and feel at ease with the cameraman; never just book over the phone. You must understand what will be involved, and he must learn exactly what you do and do not want. Book your video as far in advance as possible and remember the following:

You should see a complete recent tape before you decide—not a smart sample made to impress. Is he a professional trained cameraman? Does he have back-up equipment? Listen to the sound carefully. Does he dub over 'romantic', slushy music? Is the fee all-inclusive? Find out if there are any extras—licence, travelling expenses, etc. How much does he charge for extra copies of the video? Book only someone who can stay the whole day. Will he be suitably dressed? Give him your photographer's name so they can liaise beforehand, preventing any aggravation on the day.

VIDEO COVERAGE

The video-maker covers the salient points of the wedding in much the same pattern as the photographer. He works through the day in sequence, recording highlights of vision *and* sound to produce a coherent whole. During the course of the day, he aims to capture every guest on film. Discuss the coverage in advance, so you can leave the cameraman to get on with his task on the day.

If you are worried that it will be difficult to be sincere during the marriage ceremony with a camera whirring away, do find out exactly what equipment will be used and where it will be positioned to set your mind at rest. (Video

cameras are in fact noiseless.) Make sure that family and guests seated nearby know the form too.

Some churches require the company to have a licence from the Mechanical Copyright Society. The video-maker should ask your minister about such requirements and if he has any objections to filming in church.

If you are getting married in a register office, speak to the registrar about the form. Most allow filming before and after but not during the ceremony.

A HOME VIDEO

There's no harm in a home video, but it won't necessarily do you or the event justice. Quite apart from the need for professional expertise, it is far more successful to have an anonymous cameraman than a friend. Guests won't be so ready to play the fool in front of the camera or talk directly to the person behind the viewfinder. Friends tend to film people they know to the exclusion of other guests; they often miss highlights because they're too busy having fun. View a home video as a fun extra rather than the main record of the day.

Flowers

ABOVE

The alternative to the natural country look: a relatively contrived bouquet studded with waxy flowers and a minimum of foliage.

Flowers are a key part of the wedding, and worth planning carefully. Flowers are needed for the bride's and bridesmaids' bouquets and head-dresses; buttonholes for the groom, best man and ushers; corsages for the mothers (optional); and to decorate the church and reception. Used with thought and imagination, they can create atmosphere—vibrant and fragrant.

Of course, your pocket may not match your imagination, which leads many brides to skimp on flowers or get friends and relations to play florist. This may work for the church and marquee, but it is worth employing a trained florist to make up bouquets and headdresses. It is a time-consuming and skilled job, and one that has to be carried out immediately before the wedding when there are a dozen and one other things to have to think about.

Personal recommendation, as with all services, is the best way to choose your florist. Using a local florist is more convenient and saves delivery costs. Some, however, can be dated and unadventurous, so ask to see photographs of past work. Florists should be able to take care of the entire floral aspect of weddings. If decorating the church/reception, they will probably want to see the venue beforehand. Give at least three months' notice.

Your florist will need a visual idea of the dress to make the bouquet and headdress suitable in style, shape and colour. Take snippets of material of the dress and bridesmaids' outfits, sashes and ribbons, and drawings or photos of the designs. Discuss your hairdo for the headdress and the whole look. Florists try to suit the style of bouquet to your character, which is why a personal visit is so important. Most brides visit their florist at least twice.

RIGHT

Strong colours make a striking change from traditional whites, pinks and yellows. This bride follows the Edwardian trend of an abundant bouquet of garden roses, and a hat rather than a headdress laden with flowers.

BELOW

Table decorations do not necessarily require great skill or expense. This simple centrepiece of fruit, ivy and just a handful of roses is glorified by the container— a fine crystal bowl on a silver pedestal.

CHOOSING THE FLOWERS

You may have one or two favourite flowers plus a colour theme, which could be your starting point. Look at lots of magazines as well as the florist's portfolio; ask your dressmaker's advice and ask the florist to sketch her ideas. Consider practicalities too. What will you be happy carrying, for example? Neatly bound stems are user-friendly, but can look twee. A sheaf can be clumsy to carry, but looks fresh and countrified. Remember, too, that your bouquet has to be something your chief bridesmaid can take over easily in church.

Most flowers can be obtained throughout the year, although prices will rise dramatically out of

season. It is wise to arrange an alternative choice of flowers in case of bad weather or unavailability.

SUGGESTIONS FOR FLOWERS AND FOLIAGE

All year: Carnations, chrysanthemums, gypsophila, orchids, statice. Most evergreen foliage, with the bonus of blossoms and berries in season. Dark glossy leaves—holly, laurel, bay and cotoneaster. Variegated foliage— euphorbia and ivy (particularly Hedera 'needlepoint' and caneriensis). Ferns— asparagus, maidenhair and hare's foot. Dried foliage—ornamental grasses, reeds, seeds, pods and fruits. Herbs such as the traditional rosemary.

Spring: Azaleas, bluebells, camellias, cornflowers, daffodils, forget-me-nots, freesias, fruit blossom, grape hyacinths, heather, jasmine, lilacs, certain lilies, narcissi, primroses, sweet peas, violets. Twigs of new foliage such as small freshly opened birch leaves on the branch, lightweight sprays of mimosa, Solomon's seal.

Summer: Many of the spring flowers listed above continue to bloom and may be considered. Also buttercups, daisies, delphiniums, gardenias, guelder roses, honeysuckle, irises, certain lilies, magnolia, paeonies, rhododendrons, stephanotis, tuberoses. Natural foliage from the abundant selection of flowers in bloom. Hedgerow plants—cow parsley, elder, etc—and cottage garden sprays of lavender and golden rod.

Autumn: Heather, Michaelmas daisies, belladonna lilies. Leaves that are changing colour (for reception and church): all manner of foliage in rich shades of bronze and gold, such as copper beech and acer. Harvest fruits—wheat, barley, berries and currants. Green foliage—bells of Ireland, varieties of mahonia and hosta.

Winter: Camellias, freesias, snowdrops, Christmas roses. Conifers and shrubs such as holly, pieris (especially *Pieris japonica*) and spotted laurel give a show of colour with berries. Glossy evergreen bouquets with lipstick-red berries can be stunning against a sheeny satin dress.

Fragrance: A lovely idea is to fill your surroundings with highly scented flowers. The following should keep guests sniffing: daffodils, freesias, fruit blossom, gardenias, grape hyacinths, honeysuckle, irises, jasmine, lilacs, lilies, lily of the valley, magnolia, myrtle, narcissi, paeonies, roses, stephanotis, tuberoses and violets.

Foliage: More fashionable now than ever. Shapes vary from spikes and spires to tendrils and trails; textures from downy soft to shiny smooth; colours from silvery grey through greens and yellows to natural wheat and autumnal russet. You could work almost exclusively with foliage in winter when the selection of fresh flowers is limited.

Artificial flowers: Many brides feel happier in silk flower headdresses. Even bouquets can look good using the fine fakes available. The advantages are no wilting, no seasonal worries, no hay fever—and you can keep them. Feathers and ribbons can be incorporated. Dried flowers and leaves look gorgeous in

ABOVE

Instead of the more usual wreath or Alice band of flowers, this bride's simple headdress of white roses forms a topknot from which the veil descends.

autumn and winter, particularly at the church and reception, and, for example, carried in baskets by the bridesmaids.

THE SYMBOLIC FLOWER

Since ancient times, certain flowers and foliage have been dredged in symbolism. The Saracens connected orange blossom with fertility, for the plant is abundant in flowers, fruit and lustrous dark leaves. Still the most traditional bridal flower today, it is maddeningly difficult to obtain; yet artificial orange blossom is said to bring bad luck.

It was customary for a Victorian bridesmaid to plant a sprig of myrtle from the bridal bouquet at the bride's door. Its future blossoming heralded the next wedding, but if it died, the girl who planted it would become an old maid. Happily, myrtle propagates with ease. Cuttings of myrtle and veronica from Queen Victoria's wedding bouquet have flourished into bushes at Osborne House on the Isle of Wight, and subsequent royal brides take sprigs for luck.

THE LANGUAGE OF FLOWERS

With the Victorians, the language of flowers blossomed and flourished. Almost no flower was left unlabelled; here are the meanings of some of the most common flowers.

buttercup—childhood memories, childishness

camellia (white)—unpretending excellence; (red)—loveliness

carnation—pure love, deep love

cornflower—hope

daisy (white)—innocence

forget-me-not—true love

gypsophila ('baby's breath')—fertility

honeysuckle—bonds of love, sweetness of disposition, fidelity

ivy—friendship, fidelity, the unbreakable bond of marriage

jasmine—amiability

lily (white)—purity and modesty

lily of the valley—love charm, return of happiness

myrtle—love

orange blossom—bridal festivities, fertility, marriage luck, love

orchid—beauty

rose—love; bridal rose—happy love; white rosebuds—girlhood and a heart
   ignorant of love (the Victorian interpretation of virginity); red
   rosebud—pure and lovely; white rose—I am worthy of you

stephanotis—you can boast too much

tulip (red)—declaration of love

violet (blue)—faithfulness

Beware lavender (distrust), yellow rose (decrease of love, jealousy), striped carnation (refusal) and yellow carnation (disdain).

RIGHT

A loose shower bouquet of salmon-pink blooms with trailing foliage. The bride's headdress complements her hair-style and serves to anchor the veil.

ABOVE

The loveliest flowers are often the simplest. Here, colourful country-garden blooms— cornflowers, daisies, sweet peas and honeysuckle—are woven into a plait of glorious red hair.

THE BRIDE'S BOUQUET

'Let the flowers breathe and let the butterflies in,' said Constance Spry. If a stem swept to the right, she let it be. She never manipulated flowers into an unnatural position. Today, her influence over every aspect of floral arrangement is felt more strongly than ever.

A good bouquet should be featherlight and well balanced both in appearance and to carry. Fresh flowers should look like fresh flowers. There should be a natural, flowing movement to the bouquet rather than a static, sculpted shield of blooms, wire strangling the life out of them.

You could choose different blooms of the same colour (for example, white roses, gardenias, freesias, jasmine); or stick to one type of flower with wonderful foliage, such as full-blown roses and a mass of trailing ivy; or make a colourful splash with, say, cornflowers, poppies and roses in a riot of shades. In general, there is wider use of exotic blooms and more unusual foliage today. Movement is still crucial, be it flowing or dynamic.

The natural country look flourishes alongside the traditional romantic wedding dress. Choose wild flowers and country garden flowers such as cow parsley, clouds of gypsophila, honeysuckle, lily of the valley, pinks, roses, herbs, and twiggy and trailing foliage. Smaller blooms give a dotty, feathery, light effect; larger flowers add impact. If your dress is heavily decorative, the bouquet can be simpler.

A more understated, sophisticated dress looks good with a starker, more striking bouquet. Use a sparing selection of spectacular blooms such as orchids, arum lilies or trumpet lilies set in spiky foliage, or even just one lovely lily.

BUDGET BOUQUETS

Save florist's bills by choosing a loose arrangement—not too many blooms— of flowers that are in season. Cut costs dramatically by carrying a single flower from the garden or an armful of roses or lilies tied together with ribbon. One spring bride dressed up a bunch of daffodils with a foppish white bow. Early in the morning, after the dew has gone, gather fresh flowers from the garden or hedgerow. Choose half-closed blooms, nothing full-blown. The added advantage of flowers on their stems is that they can be kept in water until the last moment. Keep them cool and spray with water as well. As for wired bouquets, don't be deceived by the loose, natural look—they require professional construction.

BEDECKED WITH FLOWERS

Victorians used to deck the whole dress in flowers—garlanded around the hem to echo flounces and other details, and with corsages on the bodice. This could easily be done today, wiring flowers and ivy, say, into a fine garland and pinning or tacking it in swags above the hem of the dress, or wearing it as a long sash diagonally from shoulder to waist. Clusters of little flowers can be pinned on the dress, and cuffs can be encircled by flowers.

THE HEADDRESS

A fresh-flower headdress can be the bride's crowning glory. Don't be put off by the thought of it wilting: roses (though not their foliage), lilies, tuberose, honeysuckle, freesia and many other flowers will last. Some hairdressers or florists can even come to the reception and revive the headdress with fresh flowers. Just how much impact the headdress has depends on your personality.

Fresh flowers can be used in multifarious ways. Consider a frondy garland; a halo laden with large blooms; a flower tiara; a floral Alice band; slides with sprigs of flowers; a single exotic bloom gripped behind one ear in South Pacific fashion; a semi-circle of flowers at the back of the head; a dramatic evergreen wreath of, perhaps, bay, myrtle, rosemary, or ivy; flowers entwined in the hair, Pre-Raphaelite style.

A floral wreath represents maidenhood, which dies along with the flowers. The circlet, like the bride's bouquet, can be thrown among the guests—to secure a fragment ensures early marriage.

BRIDESMAIDS' FLOWERS

The bridesmaids' flowers can be beautifully spontaneous, with splashes of colour. Bouquets for grown-up bridesmaids can follow the line of the bride's, but with less extravagance and more colour. Fidgety children want nothing too cumbersome or intricate that can be strangled by hot little hands. Youngsters can't fail to look adorable with beribboned posies, baskets or trugs laden with country flowers, pomanders looped over a wrist with ribbon, hoops twisted with flowers, or one long garland fastened to the wrist of each bridesmaid—like a slave train. (This may keep them together for the service, but there will be histrionics later if you don't liberate them.)

The headdresses could echo the bride's, topknots circled with flowers, or half-circlets worn at the back of the head. Little bridesmaids could wear flowers that represent childhood innocence—buttercups and daisies—plus pretty wild flowers and cottage garden flowers such as cornflowers and honeysuckle. These less formal headdresses could be made by an amateur. Simply wire the flowers to a circlet of cotton-covered wire from a haberdashery or hat department. (Make sure it is an exact fit—an uncomfortable headdress will be discarded early on in the proceedings.) Some flowers that are prone to droop, such as lily of the valley, should have their stems plunged in boiling water. Flowers can be pinned to young bridesmaids' shoes but will not last for long.

BUTTONHOLES AND CORSAGES

It is the groom's or best man's responsibility to organise buttonholes for themselves and the ushers. Non-droop carnations are most popular, while roses, gardenias or sprigs of lily of the valley are sweeter-scented alternatives. Choose flowers in white, or to match the bride's colour scheme.

The mothers of the bride and groom sometimes each wear a corsage—a spray of flowers in a colour to match their outfit.

CHURCH FLOWERS

The first step is to talk to your minister, who is in charge of church flowers. If you are using a florist, she should liaise with the church. Volunteer flower arrangers from the parish may be happy to advise you or to assist or even take over arranging the flowers. Alternatively, a local flower arranging society might decorate the church, for just the price of materials.

Decorate the church the day before and ask the head arranger to check the flowers and top up vases on the morning of the wedding. If there is more than one wedding on the day, liaise with the other bride(s) to agree on colours and perhaps share the cost. The flowers are normally left in church afterwards.

As a general rule, place flowers high up, where light falls on them and they are most visible. A few large arrangements are better than lots of small ones, apart from posies at pew ends. Pale creamy or silvery tones are the most striking—dark colours, particularly blue, get lost. You don't have to stick to conventional arrangements. If pews face the aisle, swag garlands along the front pews. Flowers can be festooned around the font and any pillars. Line the aisle with potted fruit trees in blossom.

FLOWERS FOR THE RECEPTION

In hotels, restaurants and some hired halls, flowers will be part of the wedding package, arranged at their discretion. You should be able to choose the colour

ABOVE

Evergreen foliage dotted with assorted white roses forms a stunning entrance arch.

RIGHT

Church decorations need not be restricted to pews and pedestals. Here an unruly mass of foliage and creamy white flowers helter-skelter down solid stone columns.

autumn and winter, particularly at the church and reception, and, for example, carried in baskets by the bridesmaids.

THE SYMBOLIC FLOWER

Since ancient times, certain flowers and foliage have been dredged in symbolism. The Saracens connected orange blossom with fertility, for the plant is abundant in flowers, fruit and lustrous dark leaves. Still the most traditional bridal flower today, it is maddeningly difficult to obtain; yet artificial orange blossom is said to bring bad luck.

It was customary for a Victorian bridesmaid to plant a sprig of myrtle from the bridal bouquet at the bride's door. Its future blossoming heralded the next wedding, but if it died, the girl who planted it would become an old maid. Happily, myrtle propagates with ease. Cuttings of myrtle and veronica from Queen Victoria's wedding bouquet have flourished into bushes at Osborne House on the Isle of Wight, and subsequent royal brides take sprigs for luck.

THE LANGUAGE OF FLOWERS

With the Victorians, the language of flowers blossomed and flourished. Almost no flower was left unlabelled; here are the meanings of some of the most common flowers.

buttercup—childhood memories, childishness

camellia (white)—unpretending excellence; (red)—loveliness

carnation—pure love, deep love

cornflower—hope

daisy (white)—innocence

forget-me-not—true love

gypsophila ('baby's breath')—fertility

honeysuckle—bonds of love, sweetness of disposition, fidelity

ivy—friendship, fidelity, the unbreakable bond of marriage

jasmine—amiability

lily (white)—purity and modesty

lily of the valley—love charm, return of happiness

myrtle—love

orange blossom—bridal festivities, fertility, marriage luck, love

orchid—beauty

rose—love; bridal rose—happy love; white rosebuds—girlhood and a heart ignorant of love (the Victorian interpretation of virginity); red rosebud—pure and lovely; white rose—I am worthy of you

stephanotis—you can boast too much

tulip (red)—declaration of love

violet (blue)—faithfulness

Beware lavender (distrust), yellow rose (decrease of love, jealousy), striped carnation (refusal) and yellow carnation (disdain).

RIGHT

At the hub of the reception celebrations, the wedding cake and table are a focus for floral decoration. This table is swagged with a double row of garlands, and the white-iced cake is adorned by more fresh flowers. Note too the magnificent basket of flora.

scheme as long as there isn't another reception that day. Private houses and marquees can be decorated by your florist, your caterer, or you and your friends. One focal point is the entrance where you receive guests. The other is the cake—place a posy on top and arrangements or festoons at the base. In addition, put small arrangements on tables.

In the house, place large pedestals where they can best be seen. Garlands can be hung over fireplaces and paintings, and twisted around bannisters. In autumn and winter, swags of dried flowers, foliage and fruit look sumptuous above mantelpieces and pictures. Rich brocade can be draped as part of the design. Marquees give masses of scope for flowers—spiralling down poles, in baskets hanging from support points, festooned along the top of the tent wall, decorating chandeliers, filling stone urns, entwined in trellis work. Ornamental trees, pedestals and flower trees can also be used, and mini flower trees placed on the table.

As well as flowers, consider using fruit, vegetables, moss and lichen. Sculpted arches would look dramatic, as would topiary. An umbrella of flowers could be arranged over the top table, and mosaics of petals could be strewn in the bride's path.

RIGHT

On a lovely summer's day, a traditional canvas marquee is an idyllic setting for the reception. Tent poles can be festooned with unpretentious country flowers, creating a veritable bounty of blooms.

Dressing the Part

WHEN YOU GET ENGAGED, YOUR FIRST THOUGHT IS PROBABLY NOT, 'OOOH, I'M

GETTING MARRIED, LET'S ORGANISE THE CAR HIRE'. IT IS ALMOST CERTAINLY,

'HMMMM WHAT SHALL I WEAR?' A YOUNG WOMAN'S FANCY TURNS TO THE

DRESS, FOLLOWED BY THE ACCESSORIES, THE TROUSSEAU, AND OUTFITS FOR A

GAGGLE OF BRIDESMAIDS AND PAGEBOYS. THIS IS AN OPPORTUNITY FOR HUGE

SHOPPING SPREES AND LOTS OF SELF-PAMPERING, A TIME FOR STRETCHING

YOUR MOTHER'S PURSESTRINGS AND INEVITABLY HER PATIENCE.

The Wedding Dress and Veil

The traditional wedding dress, a magnificent full-length white affair, is largely independent of fashion and season. It is true that designers are today placing the emphasis on a narrower silhouette, with less fussily pretty, ribbons-and-bows romanticism and more beautifully cut, unadulterated classicism. Summer collections have also included a smattering of short, sharp frocks. Yet which dresses remain the biggest sellers? The fullest fairytale extravaganzas. One designer admits that the more sophisticated styles tend to make women look older and more severe, when they would rather look feminine and pretty.

And for this feminine look, there are all manner of styles of bridal wear, taking inspiration from history—from the Age of Chivalry to the Age of Celluloid. Designer creations come modelled on your heroines: a graceful Guinevere in a gown of rippling Fortuny silk pleats; an innocent young Juliet, in a waft of white muslin, with banded sleeves and long train; Madame de Pompadour, so *à la mode*, with bows down her bodice and lace ruffles galore; the S-shaped silhouette of Lillie Langtry in bustled Edwardiana; a slinky Carole Lombard in fluid Thirties satin; and, the picture of Fifties elegance, Grace Kelly in sculpted duchesse satin and lace.

CHOOSING THE STYLE

Your criteria when choosing should be to find a style that (a) attracts you, (b) suits you and (c) has originality. It may be that the perennial look of big sleeves, fitted bodice and full skirt isn't right for you. But, as one designer sighs, most English girls don't dare break away from tradition: they want to be clones. Of course, it's not the right occasion to try out a totally new style or an outrageous idea that you would normally not contemplate. And there are certain taboos: anything décolleté, diaphanous or thigh-high is out. But this is the one day when you are the leading lady, so make the most of it!

Here are a few general points about shape. The if-you're-a-beanpole-wear-horizontal-stripes school of thought is, of course, nonsense. If you're a beanpole, you're laughing—you have a model figure. The sweet English pear is more the archetype, and the late Victorians and Edwardians knew how to enhance her. The basic lines they used would flatter almost anyone: a smooth,

ABOVE

A once-in-a-lifetime occasion deserves a once-in-a-lifetime dress and veil, individually designed and made by hand. Try experimenting with your veil and hair style as this bride has done.

RIGHT

A clean-cut jacket top is softened by a skirt of frou-frou net. Many wedding dresses are enhanced by a contrast of textures and fabrics.

Many brides take inspiration from historical heroines and period wear. This drop-waisted, three-quarter-length frock is a floaty and demure alternative to the customary full, flouncy dress.

fitted and boned bodice leading into a slightly V-shaped, dropped waistline, similar to the Duchess of York's undeniably slimming dress.

A boned bodice can miraculously flatten a big bust (sometimes so flat that you need to pad it out again). A V-waist gives the impression that your waist narrows, and takes the emphasis off the hips. If you have a thick waist and big hips, never break up the line of the dress with a horizontal waistline and highly gathered skirt. Sashes are unflattering for all but the thin, as they emphasise the bust and hips. If you have a top-heavy figure with narrow hips, look to the Hollywood-style dresses that loosely drape over the top half of the body, perhaps with batwing sleeves, and smooth over a slender waist and hips.

A graceful neck and shoulders are among the most beautiful assets a girl can have. As fashion doyenne Diana Vreeland used to say, anyone can look good if they carry themselves well and extend their necks. Avoid too much fuss at the neck and shoulders. Scooped or simple round necklines are usually more attractive than sweetheart or square necklines or other harshly geometric lines.

If you have poor skin, or go red and blotchy under stress, don't expose vast expanses of flesh. No plunge necks or scooped backs, but if you don't want to be totally covered up, use lace and veiling as a camouflage.

Some girls dream of a confection of frills and flounces to rival the wedding cake. A young, reed-slim, wide-eyed bride can carry it off, but older women or those with less than model figures should go for something more understated and sophisticated.

A WHITER SHADE OF PALE

White is right and has been for centuries, signifying purity and deterring the evil eye that preys on young virgins. Very few church brides would break with such an entrenched tradition. White, nevertheless, comes in many shades. Thick creams and biscuity beiges are creeping in, while Viscountess Althorp's frock looked as if it had been dyed in tea. Recent summers have seen a wave of pallid floral chintzes, but predominantly white, as at Wimbledon, remains the

ABOVE
Breaking with tradition, this bride wears a pared-down gown that depends on the cut rather than ruffles and bows. A jacket could be worn for the service, and shoulders bared at the reception.

rule. It's wise to steer away from Ultrabrite white—it doesn't enhance any complexion, and in the silky satins (particularly synthetic ones) used for wedding dresses, it can look cheap and shiny where ivory looks sophisticated.

Register-office brides can, of course, go to town. First-time brides tend to choose a subdued version of the traditional dress, perhaps in a cream or a pastel, but the alternative is a smart outfit and hat of the going-away kind.

FLIGHTS IN WHITE SATIN

More than ever, the emphasis is on a stunning material and cut. Soft, slippery silk, wafty chiffon, scrunchy Dupion, paper or watermark taffeta, rich brocade, lustrous duchesse satin: the beauty is in the drape of the fabric and the play of light upon it. Flights of fancy take you from the warmth of winter velvet to the transparent iridescence of organza. Added interest comes in a spray of net or tulle; lashings of embroidered, crocheted or ribbon lace; and an embellishment of beading, embroidery, silk flowers or fake fur.

Natural fabrics look and feel superior to synthetics. They fall better, colours

are generally more subtle, and the texture is more delicate. If you intend to re-use your dress, natural fabrics also dry-clean and dye better than synthetics. However, there are some good imitations of silk, particularly in the heavyweight duchesse satins, and these are, of course, cheaper.

HERE COMES THE TRAIN

Most brides do want a train, even if it's only a short one. The scale of the dress is important for a church wedding, and the train adds valuable height and impact. If you're worried about tripping up or trailing it in the mud, you can have a ribbon sewn on that ties to your wrist to keep the train hitched up out of the way. Or you can have a detachable train. The Princess of Wales's crinolined extravaganza had a 7.7 metre/25 foot detachable train of ivory silk taffeta, trimmed with antique lace that was embroidered with mother-of-pearl sequins and pearls. The Duchess of York's train flowed from a fan-shaped bow: 5.4 metres/$17\frac{1}{2}$ feet of duchesse satin beaded with anchors, waves, hearts, thistles, bees, ribbons and the initial A entwined with two Ss. But neither of them could match their mother-in-law's train, a mighty 13 metres/42 feet long, when, as Princess Elizabeth, she married Prince Philip.

HAVING A DRESS MADE

If you can afford the time and money, go to a dressmaker. There is no greater luxury or confidence-giver than wearing an original dress made exclusively for you. It is the only way in which you can combine all the design details you desire without compromising your taste. A good dressmaker will ensure her creation fits like a glove and makes the absolute best of your looks.

Don't let an amateurish friend or relation make your dress. It is a formal piece of attire and you'll need the confidence of knowing it will stay the course. There are various degrees of experienced dressmaker. The 'local lady' usually works from a pattern but has a high standard of craftsmanship. If she can't make a pattern herself, she can probably adapt existing ones and could concoct your design from two or three different patterns. The professional dressmaker can cut her own patterns and will design to order, combining your ideas with her expertise. The designer-shop will normally have a collection from which you choose; then they will have the design made to measure, perhaps adapting the odd detail.

The name couturier-designer (such as Hardy Amies, Catherine Walker, Victor Edelstein, Gina Fratini, Emanuel, Lindka Cierach and Tomasz Starzewski) is a loftier version of the professional dressmaker and will probably have a team of seamstresses, emboiderers, beaders, etc. It is the work of these artisans, as well as the cut, that sets designer dresses apart.

ABOVE
Lindka Cierach, designer to the Duchess of York, is known for her lavishly embellished wedding dresses. Lace panels and frills, silk roses and intricate beading make this gown a magnificent showpiece.

DRESSMAKERS' LORE

It is supposed to be bad luck for a bride to make her own dress; even professional dressmakers often avoid making their own. The seamstress who inserts the first stitch into a wedding dress will herself be married before the year is out. Whistling in the workroom should be banned, lest it whistles up evil spirits; and tacking with black thread is forbidden for its funereal associations. The French say that a bride lives the same number of years as there are buttons on her wedding dress.

FINDING A DESIGNER OR DRESSMAKER

Choose a dressmaker who has been recommended to you and whose work you admire. Don't get bullied into agreeing to use the first dressmaker you see. Make sure her attention to detail and finishing is good—hems and stitching should be invisible, covered buttons and loops neat. You should almost be able to wear the dress inside out.

To help formulate your design, cut out all the details you like from fashion magazines and build up a file of cuttings and sketches to take to your dressmaker. The professional dressmaker will inject her ideas and knowledge, do sketches and suggest material. She may have swatches and will certainly have good sources of fabric and trimmings that she can buy wholesale. If you are using a local dressmaker, you may have to buy your own fabric. The whole process will take about four to six weeks, with about four fittings. Have your final fitting a week or two before the wedding. In general, dressmakers require at least two months' notice (four is better).

AN OFF-THE-PEG DRESS

The disadvantage of buying off the peg is finding a good fit; the advantage is an instant buy, generally though not necessarily at a lower price. Many bridal shops offer a form of couture service, where they can make to measure any design from their range. Others may be able to alter existing dresses to fit. If you are on a tight budget, brave the stores and shops at sale time, in January and July. Sale dresses will be old samples and end-of-season stock; some can look shabby, but you will get more for your money.

SECOND-HAND ROSE

You may be able to find a wedding dress agency or hire company. Agencies sell once-worn dresses at about a third of the original price, plus commission from the seller. Hire cost is also about a third of the retail price. In general, dresses are hired out only five or six times, and dry-cleaned after each wedding, before being sold—either to the last bride or cut-price in the shop.

Brides may not only choose the same sort of styles their mothers wore; some wear Mother's dress itself, cleaned and altered to fit.

TO HAVE AND TO HOLD

The golden rule is not to acquire your dress too soon; fashions, your own taste, and your size could change. More importantly, as dressmakers have discovered through experience, if the dress is ready too early, it somehow seems to lose its allure. Pace it to be finished just before the day, as part of the general crescendo of preparations.

Folklore decrees that the dress should not be completed until the actual wedding day in order not to tempt fate. The superstitious add the final stitch just before leaving for church, or, with a ready-made dress, leave off some detachable part such as a sash, even during fittings. Better advice would be to sew in a little lucky charm at the last minute. As we all know, the groom should not see his bride-to-be's dress before the wedding. (Nor should he see his bride on the morning of the wedding.)

Whether you are buying your dress or having it made, do try it on with your wedding shoes to get the length right, and be sure to match all the shades of white and cream of your dress and accessories (see pages 90–92). It would be practical to try on your full ensemble with the veil, but tiresome folklore warns that if the veil is put on before the day, the bride may be deserted, have an unhappy marriage or even die before the wedding. Should a friend try it on, she may run off with your new husband. You are even warned not to look in a mirror before you are fully dressed and your toilet completed (which, unless you have a stream of maidservants, is asking for trouble).

SOMETHING OLD, SOMETHING NEW

The old rhyme, 'Something old, something new, something borrowed, and something blue' is one of the few superstitions that most brides adhere to (although the last line, 'and a silver sixpence in your shoe' dropped off—even before decimalisation). Something old and something new represent the transition from the couple's old life to their new one. Something borrowed,

ABOVE

A register office wedding means you can dress exactly as you wish. This bride could not be further from tradition with her short, sharp frock of iridescent purple silk, her shoulders and knees exposed.

RIGHT

Every young girl's dream dress—romantic, frothy and feminine, with a contemporary twist in the form of barely-there transparent sleeves.

preferably from a happily married woman, brings marital happiness and security. Something blue signifies constancy. The Princess of Wales's dress was trimmed with old lace, the silk taffeta was new, she borrowed the Spencer family diamond tiara and diamond earrings from her mother, and she had a blue bow stitched in to her dress on the wedding morning.

TO CLEAN, PACK OR RECYCLE?

Tradition decrees that it is unlucky to sell, remodel or dye a wedding dress, lest married happiness be imperilled. Many brides like to pack the dress in a box and preserve it. In the United States thousands of brides send their dresses to a Los Angeles laboratory for ultrasonic dry-cleaning, which guarantees the dress's life for a century. It is then laid to rest in an airtight casket.

However, the more practical-minded have no hesitation in transforming their dresses into ballgowns, christening robes or camiknickers...and one bride even made her brocade dress into lampshades. It helps to justify the expense if you can get more than one day's use out of it. Dressmakers can advise you on remodelling and on dyeing a dress. Only have it dyed professionally. Natural fabrics and threads should dye consistently.

Whatever afterlife you intend for your dress, have it dry-cleaned as soon as possible after the wedding. Champagne, white wine, scent and perspiration are invisible, but will yellow with time. If you do stain your dress, the experts advise you not to touch it, but to bring it to them as soon as possible. Be sure to use a hand-finished process, which means extra care is taken, and the dress will be ironed, not machine-pressed. After cleaning, wrap the dress in tissue paper to avoid creasing and pack it in a box away from daylight.

THE VEIL

The bride's ensemble is incomplete without a cloud of veiling. Some girls profess they want to look 'natural' and so dispense with the veil, but it is a vital accoutrement. Having outgrown its original function (when it protected the bride from the wicked eye of a jealous suitor), it serves today to balance the total image, adding to the splendour and stature of the bride at this formal event. Moreover, there is the modesty and mystique of the concealed face, demure but alluring, on entering the church, and the triumph of the return down the aisle, veil thrown back and wafting on a breeze.

A good veil is not cheap. You could follow the tradition of borrowing an old veil, or look for an antique lace veil, or hire one from your dress shop. Otherwise, ask your shop or dressmaker to make your veil to match the dress. Fine silk tulle is expensive, but it is the only veiling to fall really beautifully. All you need to do is secure a doubled length on to an Alice band—good veiling needs no trimmings, though veils can be sewn with pearls or sequins. Cotton net would be suitable, but nylon really is too stiff and scratchy unless you want a dramatic spray effect. The veil may also be anchored with a tiara, or a silk or fresh-flower headdress (see page 71).

RIGHT

Swathes of drapery suggest a hint of bedouin, or a sense of classical Greece. No adornment or surface decoration exists here—the interest is all in the ruching and draping of the material.

Bridal Accessories and Trousseau

ABOVE
*Costume jewellery is just as
striking as the real thing.
These dangly pearl clusters are
ideal with a simple neckline
and upswept hair.*

The word trousseau derives from the old French 'trusse', a small bundle of valuables, originally paid to the husband. Nowadays that bundle is a bridal perk. It refers to the bride's outfits and accessories for going away and the honeymoon, plus her wedding-day underpinnings.

LINGERIE

Don't underestimate the importance of your underwear. Unless you are utterly sylph-like, you'll need to find something supportive yet pretty that won't spoil the line of the dress. Of course, if your bodice is boned, you won't need a bra. If not, the good news is that those old-fashioned contraptions are back with a vengeance. The Eighteen-Hour Girdle and the Cross-Your-Heart Bra That Lifts And Separates are not just for mothers. Figure-clenching basques and brassieres are actually *comfortable*, help posture, smooth out spare tyres and give you the confidence of knowing you'll stay in place all day.

Frilly French knickers and camiknickers are undoubtedly delectable, but best saved for the honeymoon as they can bunch up under your dress. There is nothing worse than self-evident straps, lace, dark colours or a VPL (visible panty line). Underwear must fit like a second skin; consider a strapless bra and make sure it is cut low enough at the back. Flesh, apricot or creamy tones are the least obvious under white. A heavy dress on a hot day can be punishing, so minimise the layers and wear sheer or lacy stockings or tights. (Pop socks may be practical but how unsexy can you be?) A garter is for fun and for flashing at the reception; it should be worn above the knee.

JEWELLERY

Bridal jewellery should be minimal but exquisite. Necks can look bare without some small adornment, such as a gold chain or a string of pearls. If the dress is quite plain, you could wear more stunning jewellery, but if there is already plenty of bodice detail, don't crown it with out-of-control jewels.

It is a perfect opportunity to get the precious family jewels out of the bank vaults (or at least out of Mother's jewellery box). However, if the vaults are empty and you can't borrow real jewels, don't despair—go for costume jewellery. No longer merely a copycat process, this is a trendsetting art in its

RIGHT
*Cream or palest flesh-toned
stockings are the order of the
day. Stockings hold more
allure than tights and are cooler
on a summer's day, but beware
a suspender belt showing
beneath a slim-fitting dress.*

own right. You can find lovely designs that look as fine as the real McCoy. Just avoid the vampy, gaudy, chunky looks of too much diamanté or metal.

Authentic or fake, diamonds are divine but pearls are more popular—such lustrous droplets complement the sheen of ivory silk. The prettiest pearl necklaces are a single strand or a loose choker with diamond clasp; avoid dangling ropes of pearls. There is no reason why you shouldn't wear coloured stones—either delicately hued amethysts or aquamarines, perhaps toning in with flowers and/or bridesmaids, or something bolder like sapphires or emeralds, possibly matching your engagement ring.

Earrings depend on your hairstyle and headdress. Try the whole look together before choosing. If hair is away from the ears, nothing looks prettier than diamond and pearl drops. However, the effect will be hidden with hair and earrings swinging free, so it may be wiser to go for studs or a style that clasps the lobe. Avoid anything too large and conspicuous.

Leave your hands and wrists free of chunky watches, bracelets, signet rings—stick to a fine chain or pearl bracelet and the engagement and wedding rings. Wear your engagement ring on the right hand until the wedding ring has been placed on your finger.

FOOTWEAR

Whether you splurge on a beaded extravaganza or plump for a pump, the happy day will be all the happier if your feet are comfortable. They say your feet don't touch the ground...the problem is they never *stop* touching the ground, all day long, and your feet are quite likely to swell. So be warned. Buy a style that gives support, in the correct size, and keep to the heel height you're used to (though if you're a stiletto queen, be prepared to get stuck in the grass). Do have at least a small heel—ballet shoes can be agony. Wear shoes in beforehand, and be certain they won't pinch or give you blisters after a full day's wear.

Fabric invariably looks more suitable than leather (try Scotchgarding satin against the elements), in a shade that matches your dress; most shoe shops and makers can dye. Avoid sandals and peep-toes. Several shoe designers do a made-to-measure bridal collection. Alternatively, ballet and theatrical out-fitters are a good source of shoes in modern and period styles—for example, flat pumps, court shoes with various heel heights, shoes with a Louis heel, Victorian button boots, Twenties shoes with an instep bar. Satin courts can be dressed up with ribbons, rosettes, pearl beads or silk flowers.

GLOVES

'Take away the "g" and give us a pair of loves.' Wedding guests used to exchange these words along with pairs of gloves, which symbolised maidenhood. Greek brides carry a lump of sugar in their gloves to promote sweetness all their married lives. Long silken or short lacy gloves suit certain styles of wedding dress, and gloves add glamour to any going-away outfit.

No other accessories are needed for the wedding outfit. Any items you require for the reception should be entrusted to your mother or a friend. Your purse, passport, etc, should be ready in the going-away handbag.

GOING-AWAY CLOTHES

This is your second opportunity to create a sensation with a stunning outfit. The problem with this one is that it will only be seen for about ten minutes at close quarters by the chosen few, and merely glimpsed by the majority. Choose something that is smart, striking, sharp—and photogenic. If you can wear bright colours, do. Above all, wear a hat (fashion has seldom been more accommodating to hat-lovers). Like the veil, it tops off the outfit, adds formality and helps you stand out in the crowd.

Some couples dress to complement each other: the debut of the new double act. One pair swapped roles, she departing in charcoal, he in white. Another couple went away dressed identically in his-and-hers loud grey check suits.

Hair and Beauty

For the bride-to-be, the only aspect of the wedding to receive the same attention as The Dress is its contents—The Body. A prime preoccupation in brides is with changing their appearance in some way. Yet you are more likely to feel comfortable and confident if you feel like *you*. As you will have been told a dozen times, your fiancé wouldn't have asked you to marry him if he didn't like you the way you are. On the other hand, if you don't feel at your best, it won't help the wedding photographs or your bikini'd figure on honeymoon. So if you really are concerned with losing weight, highlighting your hair and so on, then go ahead and do it.

You will probably be extra-active and a bit jittery with all the wedding preparations, so use it to your advantage to shed a few pounds. Spend a couple of days at a health spa, perhaps with your mother or your chief bridesmaid. Have a sauna or steam bath and a massage a few days before the wedding (though be careful if you are prone to spots—the steam may coax them to the surface). A facial certainly will bring spots out, so have it two weeks before. If you choose, have eyelashes dyed, legs waxed, and a pedicure in the week before the wedding. Make sure your final dress fitting is shortly before the wedding day, as your figure is bound to fluctuate.

HAIR STYLE

All sorts of people will advise you not to change your hair style just for the day. This is valid up to a point, in that you don't want to create an unknown persona for one day, but some styles are better than others with a headdress and

RIGHT

A supremely chic hair style, lacquered close to the head, with a mass of tight curls at the nape. A simple white ribbon and silk flower link the style with the dress.

RIGHT

A capricious alternative to a set floral headdress: featherlight spriggy flowers, gypsophila and white ribbon are woven into the hair in a casual fashion.

veil. In general, long hair without much body looks better worn up or back rather than straggling around your face. Styling aids like mousse, setting lotion and hairspray are a boon for fine or uncontrollable hair. Hair doesn't have to be set like polystyrene, just given extra body and structure. The Duchess of York, for example, successfully tamed her usual free-flowing mane into pretty ringlets for her wedding day.

The best policy is to try out new hair styles in conjunction with a variety of headdresses. A silk Alice band, a halo or band of silk flowers, or a tiara could form the basis of your headdress and keep both hair and veil in place. Take a few mock-up ideas along to your hairdresser, who will be able to help and advise. Some hairdressers suggest two or three trial runs before the day. For more about fresh floral headdresses, see page 71.

If you decide on a dramatic cut, colour change or perm, do it several weeks in advance so that you, your husband-to-be, family and friends can get used to it. In any case, it is good to allow a few weeks for your hair to settle down. If you are having your hair styled specially on the day, go to the salon for a run-through beforehand. Shortly before the wedding, pamper hair with a deep conditioning treatment for maximum shine.

On the morning of the wedding, either style your hair yourself (perhaps with the help of your mother or chief bridesmaid), or have it done by your hairdresser, who may be prepared to come to you. Alternatively, your dressmaker will probably be able to help with hair and headdress.

HANDS AND NAILS

Keep hands soft and smooth with a good hand cream, and look after nails leading up to the day. Keep cuticles in good condition, file nails regularly with an emery board, and wear a clear nail varnish to prevent them from chipping. Consider having a manicure at a beauty salon or your hairdresser's, either the day before or on the morning of the wedding.

MAKE-UP

Some brides have a professional make-up lesson a month or so before the wedding. But whether you have a lesson or not, it's essential to practise applying the make-up you plan to wear on the day. You'll need to aim for a natural daytime make-up rather than a party make-up with lurid blusher and heavy mascara, since unforgiving daylight exposes every bit of warpaint, and it looks garish against a sea of white.

On the other hand, bear in mind that to look your best for the camera, and particularly for video, you do require a heavier make-up. It is a tricky balance to be achieved—not too pale and washed out in all-white, yet not too colourful and artificial. A light tan gives a healthy glow to your complexion and you will need less make-up.

Here is the routine you will eventually use on the day. Apply moisturiser, allowing it to soak in for 15 minutes before putting on your base. Cover

RIGHT
Make-up needs to be natural-looking and light, with matt powder, blusher and shadows, a modicum of mascara and a soft lipstick. Make-up goes on before the final hair styling, and the dress goes on last.

RIGHT
Leave plenty of time to get ready on the day of the wedding. Not only will you be able to take essential care over your appearance, but you will be in a happier frame of mind.

blemishes and any undereye shadows with concealer, then apply foundation with a slightly damp latex sponge, to provide a good base for the rest of your make-up and even out your colouring. Make sure the shade exactly matches your skin tone, then you won't have to blend it below the jawline. Set the base and create the matt finish you need for the cameras by dusting translucent loose powder over your face with a powder puff, then brushing off the excess with a big soft brush.

Use matt, not frosted, powder eye shadows in light browns, greys or peaches. Bright colours would just look garish, and blues in particular look harsh on film. Blend the shadows well to eliminate hard edges. Use mascara and eyeliner only sparingly, preferably in brown or grey rather than harsh black. Waterproof mascara will withstand the rigours of the day better than the ordinary type, as it is less likely to run or smudge.

Match lipstick to your natural lip colour or thereabouts—warm pinks through to honey are best, and not too pale or too dark. For a lipstick with maximum staying power, choose one that's not too glossy, and apply it with a lip brush, outlining first then filling in. Applying foundation and powder, or a lipstick-fixing base, beforehand will make lipstick last longer. Blotting then powdering over the first coat of colour before applying a second is another way to ensure staying power.

Make-up artists usually put blusher on last, to avoid applying too much. Brush just a hint of powder blusher on cheekbones, beginning under the pupils of the eyes and blending outwards.

During these practice sessions, look at yourself with the headdress on, in various lights including daylight, and wearing white. You will appear quite different under different conditions.

ABOVE

Harsh daylight shows up every imperfection of make-up or skin. Even brides with a radiantly clear complexion need to be careful when applying cosmetics, being sure to blend foundation thoroughly and use muted colours.

BEAUTY ROUTINE ON THE DAY

Have a warm bath with scented bath milk, which is not as drying as foam bath, nor as oily as bath oil. Don't make it so hot that your skin becomes red or stay in for so long that you feel like going back to bed. If you are not having a professional manicure, paint nails with clear or pale pearly varnish, leaving plenty of time for them to dry thoroughly; or simply buff them up. Put on your make-up before having your hair done so that you don't spoil your hair style by scraping it out of the way—the make-up can always be touched up later.

If the hairdresser is coming to you, he or she will style your hair before you dress, and then put on your headdress and veil afterwards. Step into your dress if possible, or drape a silk scarf over your face to protect the dress from make-up smudges and then lift the dress carefully over your head with someone's help. When everything is in place, touch up your make-up, protecting your dress with a cloth if you put on any extra powder. Don't forget you will need your make-up later in the day. Put it in your mother's bag for you to use in the vestry if necessary and at the reception.

Clothes for the Bridal Party

The bride is responsible for her bridesmaids' and pages' outfits. Traditionally, her parents pay. However, it is not unusual now for attendants' mothers to pay for their clothes, or at least for material and shoes. It would be courteous to wait for the mother to offer, but if nothing is forthcoming, you could suggest sharing costs. This is an area where money can also be saved by recruiting a dressmaking friend or relation. Attendants' outfits, less formal than the bride's, should be safe in amateur hands.

BRIDESMAIDS

There are three good reasons why bridesmaids' dresses should be made specially: for the fit, as every child will be a completely different shape; for continuity, to tie in with the bride; and for style, as there is limited off-the-peg choice, particularly for grown-up bridesmaids.

It is a good idea to choose an adaptable style that can be used again as a party frock. The total look of the bridal party will be most pleasing if the line of the dresses follows the bride's, and if the colour tones in. The same creamy colour, or a deeper shade, with coloured trimmings is always successful, as are pastels. Plain fabric tends to look smarter than patterned, especially on older

ABOVE

Crisp cotton can look just as effective as more expensive fabrics. In church, all eyes will be on the back of the bridesmaids' dresses, which is why back-detailing is so important.

RIGHT

Avant-garde fashion designer Georgina Godley created the colourful costumes for her entourage at her wedding to Sebastian Conran. Dressing each little bridesmaid individually instead of identically makes a pleasing departure from the norm.

LEFT

A period theme always adds interest to the bridal party. Here a sea of Kate Greenaway girls with bonnets and baskets, accompanied by foppish artists, creates a bucolic scene.

ABOVE

Beautifully fresh and original, these bridesmaids' ensembles knock spots off some of the more staid outfits to be seen. This bride dared to eschew pink or yellow, and her black-and-white vision paid off.

bridesmaids; chintzes and silk ginghams look sweet on youngsters, but spriggy prints can look twee. In winter, you can go for richer, deeper colours. Make sure children aren't swamped by strong colours, however.

Children's dresses will almost certainly get some rough treatment, so avoid full-length frocks that would be trailed along the ground or tripped over. Use a stalwart fabric—nothing fine and chiffony that would rip. Waist petticoats are destined to slip down, so go for the type with a bodice.

PAGEBOYS

The pageboys' attire conforms to a number of set formulas. Since mid-Victorian times, it has been a tradition for small children, particularly boys, to be train-bearers. They would be got up as ruffled Little Lord Fauntleroys, wee kilted Highlanders or mini sailors—as reintroduced by the Duchess of York. All these styles are still current, particularly the silken knickerbocker story, and can be made by the bride's dressmaker to complement the bridesmaids.

Military uniforms are *de rigueur* if the groom is an officer and wearing

LEFT
Little feet—both girls' and boys'—are happy in ballet shoes, which look perfect with most summery outfits and tie in with the bride's dress.

uniform. They are available through his regiment's master tailor, who can make up miniature uniforms or lend out any he may already have.

As long as you are confident of the co-operation of your escorts, you could dress them in alternative theme wear. Since all the traditional clothing is, in effect, fancy dress, this is an area where you can be witty and original. One pair of pages came as Teddy Boys in drape coats, drainpipes and bootlace ties, with slicked-back hair; another page wore a mini maharaja outfit, a lavish brocade affair complete with turban.

CHILDREN'S SHOES

If children will be dressed in lightweight pastel outfits, they will look sweet and be comfortable in ballet pumps—and that goes for little boys (aged up to about five) as well as girls. You can embellish them with bows or silk flowers or rosettes. Heavier or darker outfits can be teamed with any plain little button shoe, perhaps of patent leather. Boys in knickerbockers or kilts should have black patent-leather buckle shoes.

THE GROOM

It's simple for the groom. *All* men look swaggeringly suave in a morning suit. It is not surprising, then, that this traditional, formal attire is back in favour with the majority of grooms. For continuity and added smartness, the best man and ushers should wear the same shade of suit as the groom.

Dark suits—black coats and charcoal trousers with a vertical pattern—are infinitely preferable to modern pale grey ones. A handkerchief should not be worn in the breast pocket: it detracts from the flower in the lapel. Waistcoats are traditionally black and single-breasted, although old-fashioned double-breasted ones in grey or buff are equally smart. Brocade waistcoats complement the sumptuousness of the bride's dress and can match in colour. Pale, stiff, single-breasted modern waistcoats are the sort most to be avoided.

A gleaming black silk top hat used to be the thing but its funereal associations have led most people to go for the grey felt variety. However, any top hat is cumbersome to carry, so it might be more sensible to dispense with it.

The shirt should be white with a stiff Eton collar (not a wing collar unless

LEFT

A work of art: exquisite hand-smocking and intricate detailing set this bridesmaid's dress apart from the run-of-the-mill. After the wedding, bridesmaids' dresses can often be worn as party frocks, much to the delight of their owners.

wearing a stock), though any plain white shirt will do; cufflinks beat buttons for dash. It's nice to break the monotony with bright braces and a jolly silk tie—coloured stripes or paisley instead of grey or black brocade. Alternatively, a stock can be worn; it looks good in creamy silk to match the bride rather than in grey cloth. Stock pins are in, tie-pins out. Feet should be clad in charcoal socks and black plain leather lace-ups.

For register-office weddings and less conventional affairs, an ordinary dark suit (or something more wacky), teamed with informal accessories, may be more appropriate than a morning suit.

MOTHERS OF THE BRIDE AND GROOM

Mothers can't go wrong if they follow the Queen's example and wear one predominant colour, a style that is unfussy and smart, and a hat which allows people to see her face. Some mothers worry about clashing with their opposite number. The bride's mother normally has first say; after deciding on the colour, she can pass the word on.

The Celebrations

THE KNOT IS TIED, LET THE CELEBRATIONS COMMENCE! THIS IS THE FUN PART—CHOOSING YOUR RECEPTION VENUE, DREAMING UP WONDROUS DECORATIONS, FINDING A BRILLIANT BAND, MEETING CATERERS OR PARTY-PLANNERS, DECIDING ON MENUS, ORDERING THE CAKE, AND STOCKING UP ON LIQUID REFRESHMENT. YOUR WEDDING RECEPTION MAY BE THE BIGGEST, MOST ELABORATE PARTY YOU EVER THROW; HERE'S HOW TO MAKE IT THE BEST, FOR YOU AS WELL AS YOUR GUESTS, SO YOU CAN CELEBRATE IN STYLE.

The Reception

Your wedding reception could be the biggest show you'll ever take part in. Let the stage be worthy of the stars. This is your chance to be different without upsetting convention. An unusual venue, exotic decoration, fun music—all these can jolly up an otherwise ordinary daytime reception. One couple spotted a skiffle band busking in the street shortly before the wedding day, and persuaded them to stroll around their reception, playing impromptu. The guests loved it and the event took on a light-hearted air.

The majority of couples, according to two recent surveys, follow their reception with an evening party. Dinner is normally provided, but you could have an after-dinner dance starting at 9.30 or 10 pm. The party is often for wild young things only, and the venue is usually the same (get full value out of that marquee).

See the section on Food and Drink, pages 114–117, for suggestions on the best time of day for your reception and party, and for information on seating and table plans.

Finding the right venue for the reception is largely a matter of logistics. It should be as near the church as possible. If you live in the country and have a fair-sized garden, you will probably want to make use of it—in which case you will need a marquee, though some couples risk a wedding in the open air. Otherwise, you may hire a local hall or house.

If you live near a river, you could hire a cruiser (look in your Yellow Pages for companies) and paddle off with your guests. Numbers in this case will be strictly limited; also, bear in mind that once you set off, everyone has to remain on the boat until disembarkation time.

BELOW

A reception is for receiving guests, and here is a receiving line of substance. It includes the entire bridal party, from the parents of the bride and groom to the couple, bridesmaids and best man.

HOTELS

The most popular venue is a hotel. In common with clubs, restaurants, boats, and museums, they take care of the whole reception—venue, decor, food, drink. It means less work for you, and it is easier to keep tabs on your budget, but it does tend to lack individuality.

A typical hotel wedding package, based on a two- to three-hour cocktail party, includes hire of reception room(s), flowers, toastmaster, changing rooms for the couple, half a bottle of champagne a head and canapés. Prices are charged per head. Musicians, bands and discos can usually be arranged.

RIGHT

The stuff wedding dreams are made of, when a flourishing garden becomes the focus of the celebrations. A conventional canvas marquee, despite certain practical disadvantages, remains the most popular type. Most tents, like this little pavilion, can have their walls removed to provide a shield from the sun rather than from the rain.

RIGHT

The setting is right and the reception is under way: your feet will hardly touch the ground as you flit from guest to guest, beaming from ear to ear.

MARQUEES

There are two types of marquee: the traditional canvas tent with one or two central poles and guy ropes; and the aluminium frame tent, a free-standing, plastic-walled structure with no ropes or poles. Most people plump for the traditional type, but a frame tent has advantages. No poles means everyone can see the action, and no ropes means guests won't trip up. You can have French windows leading into the garden and can extend the marquee directly from the house. They are safe and undraughty in high winds and wintry weather.

Whichever type of marquee you have, the lining is a matter of choice, and costs about half as much again as the marquee. It can have voluptuous ruches or wide stripes (yellow/white or pink/white are *de rigueur*) or can be pleated or plain. For a theme party, you can have painted murals instead of lining. In hot weather you can remove the walls. Flooring, at extra charge, can be coconut matting laid directly on grass, or boarded with matting or carpeting on top. Carpeting is expensive as you can only use it once. For dancing, the best surface is interlocking parquet. The marquee firm can supply chairs and tables. They will arrange lighting and heating and, if necessary, install generators.

DECOR AND LIGHTING

A daytime reception need not be commonplace. On the contrary, it is an opportunity to let your imagination run riot. Swathes of lush fabrics or clouds of muslin, backdrops painted by you and your friends, natural foliage, bundles of helium balloons—all add atmosphere. You could base a country wedding around a theme—a rustic Thomas Hardy scene, a medieval jousting party, a boating regatta. Water of any sort adds atmosphere, be it a river, fishpond or swimming pool; float water lilies or petals on a pool. Raid the countryside for resources, such as sheaves of wheat and corn, or masses of ivy to twist round tent

poles. Hang bunting; fly flags from a stripy tent; use mad props and fibreglass statues from theatrical prop hire companies.

Parties are all about creating mood, appealing to all the senses. Night-time events have a head start—a dark setting can be lit by flickering candles, fairy lights or flaming torches; scented with herbs and flowers or essences dropped on to light bulbs; filled with evocative soundtracks and music.

Colour themes are fine, but avoid matching *everything*. It's nice up to a point to be colour-coordinated, and a subtle matching of creams and ivories looks classy and thought-out.

PARTY MUSIC

Once the stage is set for your evening party, you'll need a band. Choose one that comes personally recommended, plays together regularly and is aimed at the right age-group—or is versatile. Most dance bands play a mixture of golden oldies, rock 'n' roll, current chart hits, plus Latin American, jazz,

ABOVE

Hotel banqueting facilities vary from the ordinary to the extraordinary, and lighting and decor can transform them dramatically from one occasion to the next. The Lancaster Ballroom at The Savoy Hotel in London is one of the more splendid rooms available for a wedding reception.

RIGHT

Maximising the oohs and aahs of the big day, fireworks provide a climactic finale to an already spectacular event.

Scottish reels, to suit all ages. You may want to run through their repertoire and let them know if there are any special songs you'd like played. A good band will play the right tune according to the mood of the party (and at the right volume, so that you don't have to shout). You could hire a theme band— jazz or steel, for example—and carry the theme through to the dancing. A barn dance or Scottish reels are a terrific way to get everyone involved.

If you want a band *and* discotheque, it is best to book these from the same firm so that they can work happily together. The requirements for a disco are the same as for a band, apart from an overall professionalism and efficiency. It is traditional for the bride and groom to lead the dancing. You could ask the band to commence with a song relevant to you.

CABARET AND FIREWORKS

If money is no object, why not bring on the dancing girls and send up the rockets? *Why* not? Your guests have already had one seated show today, and may well prefer to chat, dance and circulate rather than be ushered into their places again for an all-singing all-dancing spectacular. A fun alternative is a magician who moves among the crowd, performing to small groups.

Fireworks are a dazzling note to go out on. The main concern is that you have enough space for your guests to stand well back (and not be trapped inside the marquee), and can cordon off the area where the fireworks are being let off. Coordinate this yourselves or through a friend, or go to a specialist company.

THE TOASTMASTER

A toastmaster is not really necessary except at a large formal do, when you need the names of all the guests called out. Otherwise, the head waiter or the best man can announce the cake-cutting, the speakers and the going-away.

Highland hooley: the Scots know how to celebrate in style. Not for them the brief afternoon reception—this party, held in a magnificent frame tent, kept guests reeling into the night.

PARTY PLANNING SERVICES

Party planners will organise any or every aspect of your wedding, reception and/or engagement party. Matching their experience, contacts and time to your budget, they can make the whole event run smoothly. They are invaluable to those trying to arrange a wedding from a long distance or at short notice, or who just don't have the time themselves. They are not for those who want a strong hand in the planning themselves.

Planners have trade contacts that you could never get access to yourself and they can get wholesale prices on champagne and suchlike. The money saved on bargain buys will often cover the planner's fees. They can advise you where to economise and where not to, offer ideas, and take the headache out of organisation. But beware . . . despite what planners may say, costs can mount. Most, though not all, charge for consultations, secretarial work and travel, and prices may increase for work undertaken outside office hours. Make sure you are aware of all costs you may be liable for. Note that there is a difference between the middle-man planner (usually called Party Something) and those attached to catering/disco/marquee businesses; the second type is less likely to charge a consultation fee.

Food and Drink

Whether you celebrate your nuptials with nibbles, noggins or a Bacchanalian feast, the food and drink are certainly among the most important aspects of your wedding. Don't forget that, above all, a wedding has to be a good party. Better to have fewer guests than not enough to eat and drink.

The factors determining your style of catering are budget, the number of guests and the time of the wedding. If the guest list exceeds 100 or so it is wise to use an outside caterer, unless you are a professional with plenty of staff on hand. If your budget and numbers are modest you could prepare the food yourself with the help of trusted friends.

TIME OF DAY

The time of the wedding corresponds to the type of reception you wish to have and can afford. An afternoon cocktail party with bite-sized food is generally cheaper than a full lunch or dinner.

Morning marriages could be followed by a wedding breakfast or brunch of, say, scrambled eggs, kedgeree, devilled kidneys, hot croissants, Buck's Fizz and steaming real coffee. In practice, this only works well for a small party, as scrambled eggs for 200 will be unpalatably hard and watery, croissants soggy, and so on. There may be a sense of anti-climax for guests who have travelled a long way if the party ends at lunchtime. But if the catering is reliable, and it's a small, informal crowd, brunch is a scrumptious, inexpensive alternative.

If you marry around noon, lunch is on the menu. Increasingly popular and one of the most successful options, it is hampered only by budget and space. There is a focal point to the party, and everyone departs feeling well wined *and* dined. It avoids rushed pre-wedding lunches and guests getting over-drunk (too much alcohol on an empty stomach). Lunch could be a sit-down affair or a buffet; or it could be somewhere in between, with starters on the table, a buffet main course, and a served dessert. Hotels tend to cater for sit-down lunches with a top table, seating plan and full service. The ideal arrangement could be a relaxed buffet lunch. Reserve a few tables only, leaving guests to sit where they please. Instead of having one serving table at the end of the room or marquee, place smaller serving tables around the edges, with enough food for about four guest tables on each.

The traditional reception, and one that is recommended by many for economy's sake, is an afternoon cocktail-cum-tea party. Lasting two to three hours, with plenty of drink and canapés, it is short and sweet. The only disadvantage is that it can leave guests rather drunk and disorientated at an

RIGHT

Food does not have to be elaborate or artfully presented as long as everything is fresh and plentiful. Plump for whole cheeses, savoury terrines, platters of cold meat, baskets of rolls, big bowls of salad.

awkward time of day. But it does mean the bride and groom can depart for their hotel, change and have dinner in an unhurried fashion. Guests can make their own arrangements to go out to dinner somewhere nearby.

If you plan a dance, the mid-afternoon wedding slot is not the best. Seasoned guests think there should be no gap between wedding and dance because everyone feels deflated and tired by evening. It also means you are giving two parties in one day, and plying people with drink twice.

A late-afternoon wedding is ideal in combination with an evening dance, with drinks after the ceremony and then dinner. A drinks-only reception works well in London, where most guests live locally, but it isn't very suitable for country weddings where guests have travelled a long way and may have to stay in the neighbourhood overnight. Dinner with no dance suggests a degree

of formality and haute cuisine—impressive but expensive. The most obvious venue for this would be a hotel, restaurant, club or large private house, rather than a hall or marquee. A buffet is usual if there is a dance as well.

TABLE PLAN

Seating is a skilled art. It's like a dinner party 15 times over. Done conscientiously, it can make the reception an unqualified success. Done carelessly, it can leave guests bored and disgruntled. People want to feel secure with people they know, and stimulated by others they don't know. Jumble a handful of old and young from both sides of the family, but try to match like-minded people. Combine fixed seating with a degree of informality so that guests feel they can visit friends at another table. To add variety you could order all the men to change tables after the main course. Pin up a plan with everyone's table number for parties of up to 100 guests. Larger parties mean congestion around the table plan, so have several copies pinned up, or give each guest a card with their table number on it when they arrive.

At an informal reception, you could reserve just a few tables near the action

LEFT

A garden setting for a summer's wedding feast, where fruit and flowers (not to mention a bottle of champagne) are a picture in themselves.

(ie the cake) for the bridal party and VIPs, particularly aged ones. Don't lay tables, just put tablecloths on and have knives, forks, napkins and plenty of chairs readily available.

Avoid having a top table facing the reception with the bridal party in a row— no one can mix, and young bridesmaids and pages often find themselves next to unknown grown-ups. Round tables are infinitely preferable for one and all.

CATERERS

Good, experienced caterers are a boon. Not only will they take all the hassle of providing victuals off your hands, but more often than not they will have the knowledge and contacts of a party planner and will impart the information for free. A few caterers charge extra for their party-planning service.

It is most important to shop around for your caterer. Personal recommendation has to be the best introduction, but you need to obtain several estimates anyway. Request a detailed breakdown of charges, since they can cover any combination of services such as delivery, overtime, tips, service charge, equipment hire, corkage, travelling expenses, party planning.

Here is a checklist of things to ask. Do they provide all staff and will they be uniformed? How many staff will you need? Will they stay if the reception runs over the estimated time? Will they expect to be paid directly after the reception? Exactly how much food is included in the price? Do they re-plate left-over food for you, or take it away? Will they need access to kitchen facilities and for how long? If in a marquee, will they need a water supply and a service tent? Do they provide all equipment, such as tables and chairs, table linen, crockery, cutlery, cake table/stand/knife (even if they are not supplying the cake), glasses, bar equipment, ice? How long will they take to clear up? Are they known to leave everything in excellent order?

SELF-CATERING

If the numbers are manageable and you have a reliable, keen team of helpmates, you and/or your mother could organise and prepare the catering for your wedding. The golden rule is to make a detailed plan of action and to delegate the duties from stage one, so that everyone knows exactly what is expected of them. Make a countdown checklist, and stick to it rigorously.

You will almost certainly need to borrow or hire such items as cooking equipment, china, cutlery, extra chairs, an urn for boiling water, and heated trays. You may also have to book fridge and freezer space with the neighbours.

Have staff posted to serve, clear and wash up on the day. Unless the reception is at home, it may be wise to stick to cold food. If you are having hot food, delegate all kitchen duties. Your mother, as hostess, must be free to

introduce guests at the reception. For cocktails and buffets you'll need people in the kitchen, others handing food round, and still others manning the bar and buffet table. Have each course cleared and washed up as it is finished.

For stand-up afternoon cocktails, you require 0.65 square metres/7 square feet per guest; a staff-to-guest ratio of one to 20; one-half to two-thirds bottle and about 14 canapés a head. For a sit-down buffet lunch, you need 1.5 square metres/15 square feet per guest; a staff-to-guest ratio of one to 20; two-thirds to one bottle a head. For a sit-down served dinner, you require 1.5 square metres/15 square feet per guest; a staff-to-guest ratio of one to 10; and two-thirds to one bottle a head.

Don't be too ambitious. Avoid elaborate dishes from your French cookery books; choose nothing too rich, spicy, sauce-ridden, complicated or over-decorated—just good, fresh, top-quality food in ample quantities. Test out any new recipes beforehand, and work out quantities carefully.

FINGER FOOD

A finger buffet is the most informal arrangement and gives you scope to try all manner of canapés. This is no soft option—a good deal of care needs to be taken. As guests will be standing while they eat, probably without plates, food should be one-bite-sized, non-drip and non-crumbly.

ABOVE

The invariably rock-hard icing on the cake makes it difficult to cut at the best of times. Some couples skirt this problem by having the cake cut in advance, and a thin layer of icing replaced.

Hot little quiches, tartlets, baby pizzas, choux puffs, filo parcels filled with feta cheese, stuffed mushrooms, herby sausages, scampi, chicken satay sticks and so on are delicious provided they are served at the right temperature and have enough filling/dip. Successful cold finger food includes asparagus wrapped in fine brown bread; cream cheese wrapped in ham or smoked salmon; dates filled with cream cheese and walnuts; crudités (carrots, cauliflower, cucumber sticks, baby tomatoes) with dips such as taramasalata, houmos, and fresh mayonnaise; wedges of brie; peeled jumbo prawns and crab claws with dip; tiny, springy-fresh sandwiches; mini meringues; éclairs; Florentines; brandy snaps—the list is endless, and the message is freshness.

BUFFET LUNCH

Lunch is more straightforward. You can't go wrong with a cold buffet—a whole salmon, joints of ham and rare beef, turkey, a variation of coronation chicken, quiches, savoury mousses, plus easy-to-eat salads. Don't do more than one or two main-course dishes—the more variety, the more wastage. Follow with strawberries and cream, biscuits and cheese, coffee, tea. The advantage of a hot meal is you can make casseroles in advance, freeze them, then just heat them up on the day. With them you could serve salads, rice, pasta and/or hot bread. You could even ask friends to provide a dish each.

A QUESTION OF BUBBLES

Some people wouldn't dream of throwing a wedding reception without champagne, and champagne alone. This would normally be for a drinks-party reception; still wine is usually served with a meal. You could have both champagne and wine on tap (one caterer finds about a quarter of the guests

choose wine). Pink champagne is *très à la mode*. Other party-givers offer still wine throughout the reception, but insist on champagne for the toasts. For others, *méthode champenoise* or sparkling wine is perfectly respectable.

There are some fine sparkling wines available, but do choose carefully. Avoid cheap, sweet, fizzy wines which taste like Lucozade and will induce throbbing hangovers. Good, interesting sparkling wine buys are Clairette de Die, Crémant de Bourgogne Rose, and G.F. Cavalier Blanc de Blancs Sec. Another alternative is to serve Buck's Fizz, kir royale or peach fizz, mixing the orange juice or liqueur with a dry sparkling wine instead of champagne.

For a drinking wine, a light, fruity, non-acidic, medium-dry German or Alsace white goes down well, or a crisp Sauvignon Blanc. New World wines are fashionable but generally more expensive. You may want something drier, plus a red wine, to go with food.

At a winter wedding, you could have a hot punch or mulled wine on arrival, which warms the cockles and weakens the knees, followed by wine. At an evening party, you could offer spirits. Always have soft drinks available, particularly mineral water and pure orange juice.

DRINK HINTS

When ordering through a caterer, compare wine prices—it could well be more economical to buy your own, though you may have to pay a corkage fee. Clear this with your caterers and make sure they will provide ice, glasses and bar equipment. If you are going to have a pay bar, find out whether the caterer has a licence to sell drink. They should organise the licence themselves, and get an extension if you are having a late-night party.

If you are arranging your own drink, most off-licences will provide wine on a sale-or-return basis and many will hire out glasses too. If you have champagne or white wine, you will need plenty of ice (from the off-licence, or see your Yellow Pages) and somewhere to put it.

The general rule for quantity is half a bottle a head for a stand-up reception, and up to double that for a sit-down meal: people drink more with food and when they are sitting down. There is no need to skimp on alcohol if you can return unused bottles. Experience, on the other hand, shows that the more drink, the more is drunk. Things run more smoothly if wine is handed round rather than freely available at a bar. If you do have a bar, make sure you have a responsible ally behind it. Serve white wine in goblets and champagne in tulips so that waiters can top up appropriately without forever having to inquire which one a guest is drinking.

THE CAKE

'Society cakes,' proclaimed the *Tatler*, 'unlike Society brides, are dressed in white, stark-white.' You can take a colour theme too far. But white trimmed with pale pink roses or peach icing swags, or a buttery cream to match your dress, could hardly offend. Square or round in three tiers is the norm, leaving room for a little or a lot of creative licence. The cake and its table are customarily further adorned with fresh flowers.

In calculating the size of cake, remember that an extra layer is usually made for cutting before the reception, to avoid a delay in handing it round, and that it is traditional to save the top tier of the cake for the christening of the first baby. (If you completely seal it in aluminium foil and then in an air-tight tin, it will keep for many years.) As well as accounting for guests at the reception, don't forget absent friends to whom you may want to send slices (you can order cake boxes from a stationer).

A HOME-MADE CAKE

Your mother or a friend may be able to make your cake (it is supposed to be bad luck to make it yourself), but do ask a professional to ice it. Start about three months in advance of the day, since a rich fruit cake, regularly laced with brandy or another spirit, will mature irresistibly. Two to three weeks before the wedding, it's time to cover the cake with almond paste and, a few days later, to start icing, which is a skilled business. Estimate 18–22 portions per kg/eight to ten portions per pound of cake.

LEFT
The croquembouche, *a cone
of cream-filled profiteroles with
a caramellised sugar glaze,
is traditionally served at
French weddings.*

Instead of the conventional two-tier or three-tier cake, you could consider sculpting it into a shape to do with you and your fiancé's life/work/interests— for example, your house, car, boat, a clapper board, a champagne bottle.

WEDDING CAKE LORE

To taste the cake before the wedding will cause a bride to forfeit her husband's love (though whether this applies to dipping into the raw mixture, we do not know). The bride must cut the cake, with the groom's help, or she will be childless. She should then preserve some cake, to ensure her husband's lifelong fidelity. And for luck, the couple should exchange and eat a morsel, after which every guest must join them in eating the cake. Single guests should sleep with a piece of cake under their pillow to dream of their future spouse. A bridesmaid who carries a piece of wedding cake in her pocket until the honeymoon is over will soon marry. After the first wedding in a family, part of the cake should be kept in the house until all the unmarried daughters are wed or they are destined to be spinsters.

The Day

AT LAST, THE DAY IS HERE, THE CULMINATION OF ALL THOSE MONTHS OF PREPARATION. YOUR CHECKLIST HAS BEEN CHECKED AND RECHECKED, AND THE DAY WILL RUN LIKE CLOCKWORK. YET, NO MATTER HOW MANY TIMES YOU HAVE RUN THROUGH THE ACTION IN YOUR MIND, NOTHING CAN PREPARE YOU FOR THE ACTUAL EVENT. YOU WILL BE PICKED UP BY A WHIRLWIND, WHISKED TO CHURCH, FLASHED THROUGH THE PHOTOGRAPHS, SPUN AROUND THE RECEPTION FROM GUEST TO GUEST, AND DEPOSITED IN A DAZED BUT HAPPY HEAP IN YOUR HONEYMOON HOTEL.

The Course of the Day

Although the wedding day is a piece of precision engineering, when the big day dawns the best policy is to relax and trust that all the component parts will slot together in the correct order at the right time.

BEFORE THE SERVICE

All major worries such as last-minute flower arranging, assembly of the cake and laying out food should be delegated to helpmates on the big day. For the immediate families, there should be nothing more flustering than getting ready and getting there. Depending on the time of wedding, do set aside some time to eat before you go. Most brides find they don't get a chance to eat at the reception, and you could find yourself going without food all day. Meanwhile, the best man will probably have been staying or lunching with the groom. The two should aim to arrive at church 20–30 minutes before the service. The ushers will have arrived 30–40 minutes before the ceremony.

Back at your parents' home, the bridesmaids and pages turn up (though the chief bridesmaid has probably been with you all morning), their car arrives, and off they go. Your mother may accompany them or go separately, perhaps escorted by other members of the family. That leaves you and your father, who will be assiduously clock-watching.

The most frequent thing to be forgotten is the bouquet. It is usually sitting somewhere in a box, keeping cool; Mother's already left and Father's in a panic. Even the veil gets forgotten. So make sure you are ready by the time your mother departs, so that she can perform the final inspection. Now is a good time to swap your engagement ring over to your right hand.

Off you go with your father and plenty of time to spare. Many's the bride who arrives 15 minutes early, and then has to circle round the block ten

BELOW
Best friends: the ideal best man is one the groom can trust implicitly, since a good deal of responsibility rests on his shoulders.

RIGHT
The bride arrives at the church with a few minutes to spare, allowing time for one or two photographs and for the bridal party to assemble.

times like an aeroplane stacking to land. In a town with congested traffic, there is little you can do to avoid this—better to arrive in good time than too late, even if you do keep passing your guests with a queenly wave.

The car draws up with a few minutes in hand. The blur begins. The click, whirr of camera and video; demure, veiled smiles at late guests; less demure adjustments to your attire; lining up attendants (pages and little maids all in a row behind the bride, the chief bridesmaid bringing up the rear); father with gritted teeth, pacing. As you enter the portals, the first bars of your familiar processional music strike. Then you launch up the aisle on your father's right arm, slowly, steadily, to the chancel steps, where you fall into line to the left of the groom and best man.

THE CEREMONY

You turn and give the bouquet to the chief bridesmaid, or, if you have only small attendants, to your father, who in turn passes it to your mother. The marriage service ensues. The groom and then the bride are asked if they will take each other as wedded wife and husband, and each answers, 'I will'. When the minister asks who giveth this woman to be married to this man, your father silently takes your right hand and offers it to the minister, who passes it to the right hand of the groom. Your father can now stifle a sigh of relief and rejoin his wife in the front pew.

Soon it's the best man's moment of glory: the minister offers an open prayer book, upon which he places the wedding ring(s), which is/are blessed. The best man (and attendants if you wish) may now fall out and take their allotted pew. After the vows and exchange of rings, the couple follow the minister to the alter for prayers. There may be an address before or after the prayers, winding up with a quick word about stacking extra chairs at the back and donating generously to the fund for the church roof. The ceremony culminates with a hymn and the blessing.

The minister, you and the groom, your parents, the attendants and the best man disappear into the vestry to sign the register. Now you lift the veil back off your face (and can touch up your make-up as your kit should be in your mother's bag). Then it's time to march back down the aisle (not too fast, as the congregation are dying for a proper look at you), the beaming bride on the groom's left arm followed by a crocodile of small attendants, the chief bridesmaid and best man, the bride's mother and groom's father, and the groom's mother and bride's father.

THE RECEPTION

You emerge into the sunlight for snaps and congrats, and then bundle into the car or carriage bound for the reception. The best man, bridesmaids and pages follow in the next car, and both sets of parents hasten to the reception to take up position in the photographs and/or receiving line before guests arrive.

The time will flash past for you and the groom, but it can seem a long day

RIGHT
Framed by a glorious arch of foliage and white blooms, the couple kneel at the altar for the prayers.

for the guests. It is the only social occasion when there is no natural hostess who knows all the guests and introduces them. The best receptions are short, sharp and to the point. A standard afternoon party should be no longer than two to three hours: for example, the wedding at 2.30, the reception at 3.30 and the departure at 6.00. The atmosphere loses its spark if the bride and groom don't go—and when they have gone it's time for the guests to go.

RECEIVING LINE

The advantage of a receiving line is that you can be sure you have greeted everybody, and guests in turn will feel they have paid their proper respects. The standard formal receiving line consists of first the bride's mother and father, then the groom's mother and father, next the bride and groom and finally (optional) the attendants. However, to avoid long queues, current trends include: (a) to cut the line down to bride and groom only; (b) for there to be two rooms—the first for guests to mingle and start partying, the second for the receiving line, cake and main reception; (c) for the bride and groom to stand near the back of the reception hall or marquee, so that guests can go up to the couple in their own time; (d) on a fine day, for the line to be at the entrance so that people can mingle outside first. If you absolutely can't avoid a queue, make sure that everyone in it is served with champagne, and that no one is left standing out in the rain.

ABOVE

Spirits are exultant as the couple stride down the church path, accompanied by a merry band of buskers.

SPEECHES

You should, without exception, stick to the convention of having speeches, however informal or short the actual speeches may be. The wedding needs a focus—the three speeches, toasts and cake-cutting—and there are people who will be offended if they are not thanked. Brevity is paramount, but there will be a general feeling of being short-changed if there aren't a few anecdotes and jokes, particularly from someone known to be a good orator.

The first speech: Proposing the health of the bride and groom, this speech falls to the bride's father, uncle, godfather or an old friend of the family. This one is about the bride, and is best kept brief, straight and affectionate; no jibes, and only witty if he is a good speaker. If the bride's father and/or mother is dead, it is appreciated to mention them and how proud they would have been. It ends with the toast: 'The bride and groom'.

The second speech: This is delivered by the groom, who proposes a toast to the

ABOVE

*Not only his-and-hers
rickshaws, but his-and-hers
coolies—a novel form of
wedding transport from a
theatrical prop hire warehouse.*

bridesmaids and pages. The toast is preceded by a chain of thank-yous,
particularly to the new parents-in-law. The tone of this speech is straightforward and sincere, with the odd light touch. It ends with the toast: 'The
bridesmaids and pages'.

The final speech: The best man's reply 'on behalf of the bridesmaids' is
traditionally a vehicle for rattling a few of the groom's closeted skeletons. If
the best man is a confident speaker, it can be very funny. If not, it can be
embarrassing and in bad taste. He should avoid a complete character
assassination, past girlfriends and general vulgarity, and should not speak for
too long. Props can be fun—but no more than one or two. It was customary
for the best man to read out telegrams, but since telemessages just don't have
the same ring, this formality is often dispensed with. Otherwise, it's best to
read out some of the amusing (but not private) messages or simply list
the well-wishers. There is no formal toast, but guests usually raise their glasses
again to the bride and groom, or to absent friends.

CAKE-CUTTING

Together the bride and groom hold the knife (upside-down for luck and a
wish) and *smile* for the photos as they slice. Easier said than done—these cakes
are like rock. You could do as the Queen did: a section was cut in advance, tied

with a ribbon and iced over. At the cake-cutting, she and Prince Philip were guided by the ribbon and only had to sever the icing. The show-cake is then whisked away and another, ready-cut replica brought in for the guests.

RIGHT

Departing in a carriage which, in character with the rest of the wedding, is awash with flowers. Happy waves from one and all, at the end of a happy day.

GOING AWAY

It's up to the best man to round you up at a pre-arranged time to go and change. You will be ravenous, so it's a good idea to arrange for a tray of food and champagne to be in your changing room. One couple's second pitstop after departing (the first was to clean the windscreen) was to buy crisps and peanuts for the journey to their hotel.

The best man should bring down your suitcases to the car in advance, before the crowd has gathered. He must also notify, loudly, all the guests that you are about to leave. So, everyone in position? Time to make your second grand entrance (and exit) of the day. Throw your bouquet if you want to (ideally from a staircase): the girl who catches it will supposedly become the next bride. Then—prepare to be mobbed.

Confetti, spaghetti, streamers, shaving foam, crazy foam—crazy guests. How do you contain them? A shower of confetti is all very well until it rains or gets into contact with the champers; then the cheap dye will run and could stain your outfit. Shaving and crazy foam are thoroughly unpleasant if you get a mouthful or an eyeful, and they too can stain. Hurling rice—an ancient fertility ritual—is little better as it stings like hail pellets. A harmless and pretty (not to mention ecological) alternative is to provide big baskets of fresh petals from overblown roses.

Caterers and planners say they've seen many a happy wedding spoilt at this stage, when the going-away vehicle appears with its dubious decorations by misguided guests. These can be not only irritating but positively harmful or dangerous. If you go away by boat, helicopter, balloon, etc, you avoid the horror, because—you hope—no one would dare sabotage them. If you have a hired car, a watchful chauffeur should be able to deter vandals. Otherwise keep your car under lock and key until the last minute, and let it be known that if the groom finds the car foaming at the windows, he will foam at the mouth. The best man and ushers can spread the word among the guests. Curbing hooligan tendencies is not a case of spoiling their fun, it's a case of not spoiling your day. There are harmless alternative ways to decorate the car—balloons, streamers, a sun visor with the couple's nicknames. Alternatively, depart in a ready-mutilated old banger and have the real car hidden somewhere nearby.

If the reception is at home, the best way of encouraging guests to leave is for the bride's parents to stand on their doorstep and not go back inside. If the reception is in a hotel or hall, the hosts are not obliged to stay until the last guest departs.

EVENING PARTY

If you're having a party later that evening, the advice for encouraging guests to go is even more applicable. Your parents will be ready for a break. For you, the

usual routine is to 'go away' to great fanfares as normal, relax and change at a nearby hotel, and then return a little after the appointed party hour. You are not expected to be present in advance to act as hosts—you are guests of honour. So make a dramatic star appearance after most of the other guests have arrived. After the dance, you go away for the second time (more tears, hugs, waves), back to your hotel.

Some couples can't keep away, and make another appearance at lunchtime the next day—particularly if friends are staying in the area for the weekend. A lazy outdoor lunch or picnic may be planned—anything to make inroads into the quantities of rice salad and coleslaw left over from the reception—or perhaps a country pub lunch, plus a little gentle opening of wedding presents. Then, you can go away for the third time, getting full mileage out of your wedding weekend, and finally head for the airport.

Wedding Checklist

Here is a complete chronological checklist of all that has to be done when organising a wedding. By each point there is an indication of who is responsible for arranging it (**B** = Bride; **M** = Bride's Mother; **G** = Groom) and which pages give further information.

ON GETTING ENGAGED

- Choose an engagement ring and possibly wedding ring. **B + G**. See pp 13–17.
- Get ring(s) insured. **G**.
- Buy a present for the groom (optional). **B**. See p 17.
- Place announcement in the newspaper(s). **B/M**. See p 12.

6 MONTHS BEFORE

- Speak to your minister, priest, rabbi or registrar and agree a date and time for the wedding. Book church/register office. **B + G**. See pp 24–31.
- Put arrangements for any special licence in motion. **B + G**. See p 25.
- Book the hotel/marquee and caterer/party planner. If wedding is at home, plan a site meeting for marquee/lighting/decor. **B/M**. See pp 108–113, 117.
- Choose your attendants—bridesmaids, matron of honour, pages (**B**), best man and possibly ushers (**G**). See pp 36–39.
- Decide on the number of guests; make list over next 3 months. **B + G**. See p 44.
- Book your honeymoon and the hotel for your honeymoon night. Arrange travel insurance at the same time. **G**.

5 MONTHS BEFORE

- Order cars/horse-and-carriage for going to the church (**B** and **G** make separate arrangements) and between the church and reception (**B/M**). Book going-away transport (**B/G**). Or make firm arrangements to borrow cars from friends or family. See pp 50–53.
- Book photographer and video-maker. **B/M/G**. See pp 54–63.
- Plan your wedding present list. **B + G**. See p 48.

4 MONTHS BEFORE

- Order wedding invitations and cake boxes. **B/M**. See pp 44–47, 122.
- Book florist. Discuss flowers for church, reception, bouquets, headdresses and buttonholes. Arrange subsequent site meeting for church or reception flowers if necessary. **B/M**. See pp 64–75.

- Order cake (home-made cake, see below). **B/M**. See p 122.
- Start planning your wedding dress and accessories, and the attendants' clothes. Book dressmaker. Book shoemaker if applicable. **B + M**. See pp 77–93, 100–103.
- Book dressmaker and milliner, if required, for going-away outfit. **B/M**. See p 93.
- Choose and buy wedding ring(s) if not already done. **B + G**. See p 17.

3 MONTHS BEFORE

- Plan music for the ceremony. Talk to the organist and choir. Book any extra musicians/choir that are not attached to the church. **B + G**. See pp 32–35.
- Have second meeting with minister and arrange rehearsal near the day. Arrange pre-marriage course if it's a Catholic wedding. **B + G**. See p 28.
- Order service sheets. **B + G**. See p 28.
- Confirm in writing choice of food and drink with the caterer or hotel. **B/M**. See pp 114–122.
- Home-made cake: commence rich fruit cakes. **M**. See p 122.
- Confirm in writing flowers with florist. **B/M**. See pp 64–75.
- Check passports are in order if going abroad for honeymoon. **B + G**. Complete post office forms if you want a new passport carrying your married name for your honeymoon. **B**.
- Make any general legal arrangements (making a Will, etc). **B + G**.
- Start shopping for going-away and honeymoon outfits and for any special lingerie, shoes, etc. **B**. See pp 90–93.
- If marrying in a register office or in a church other than the Church of England, give notice of marriage to superintendent registrar. **B + G**. See pp 30–31.

2 MONTHS TO 6 WEEKS BEFORE

- Self-catering: make thorough plan, start cooking for freezer. **B + M**. See pp 118–119.
- Plan floral decorations if doing them yourself. **B + M**. See pp 72–73.
- Buy presents for the best man and attendants. **G**. See p 36.
- Send out invitations. **B/M/G**. See p 47.
- Make a list of guest acceptances and refusals as they arrive. **B/M**. See p 44.
- Send thank-you letters for wedding presents as they arrive. **B + G**. See p 48.
- Arrange stag and hen parties. **B/G** with **chief bridesmaid/best man**.

1 MONTH BEFORE

- Book hairdresser/manicurist. Test hairstyle with headdress and veil and hat for the day. Buy any new make-up and practise. Go to beauty classes/health spas now. **B**. See pp 94–98.
- Inform caterer of the final number of guests. **B/M**.
- Prepare table plan and place cards if required. **B/M**. See pp 116–117.

- Check that the groom has organised the ring, his outfits and the honeymoon. **B + G**.
- Buy each other's special wedding present. **B + G**.
- Write to inform any official bodies of your new surname—driving licence, car registration, AA, insurance policies, building society, bank, cheque book, cheque card, credit cards, etc. **B**.
- Start wearing in wedding shoes. **B**. See p 92.

FINAL WEEK

- Have stag and hen parties (*not* the night before the wedding). **B + G**.
- Prepare flowers if you are decorating the church/reception yourselves. **B/M**. See pp 72–73.
- Check all your wedding clothes and try on the whole outfit with shoes and underwear. **B**.
- Groom to prepare his speech. **G**. See p 132.
- Have a full rehearsal at the church with all attendants. Make seating plan for church and give to head usher. **B + G**. See p 29.
- Check service sheets have been delivered to the best man for him to take to church on the day. **B/G**.
- Check timing of travel to the place of marriage (allowing extra time for your timetable). **B + G**.
- Make a final check on arrangements for caterers, cake, transport, flowers, photography, video, for exact timing and so on. **B + M**.
- Check that you have everything for your honeymoon. Pack suitcase the day before. **B + G**.
- Go to any last-minute hair/beauty appointments. **B**. See p 94.
- Lay out or hang up your underwear, hosiery, dress, shoes, make-up, jewellery, headdress and veil the night before so that you don't forget anything. **B**.
- Make a plan of action for the day. Decide where you are dressing if not at home, transport logistics (see pp 52–53), etc. **B + G**.
- Based on the checklists shown below, make out personal checklists for each member of the wedding party. Plan the timetable with your parents. The groom should make his own timetable for the wedding morning. Work around the fixed plot points. For example, hair and photographer's appointment; cars' departure for church; the service; speeches and cake-cutting; going away. See pp 36–41 for checklists for the chief bridesmaid, best man and ushers. **B/M/G**.

THE DAY

The bride

- Beauty routine.
- Hair appointment if applicable.
- Check safe delivery of your flowers.

- Dress (with chief bridesmaid's help).
- Have honeymoon suitcase suitably packed, and going-away outfit ready (don't forget hat, shoes, handbag), to be taken to the reception if it is not being held at home.
- Make sure travel documents are in a safe place.
- Photographer/video-maker's appointment, if applicable.
- When ready to leave, don't forget headdress and veil (which should be down over your face), and bouquet.
- Swap engagement ring to right hand.

The bride's mother
- Should have handed over all organisational responsibilities for the day. If not, may need to make last-minute touches to flowers, cake, food, etc.
- Arranges display of wedding presents (in practice she may do this the day before, or delegate the task).
- Keeps bride and household on schedule.
- Leaves house before bride and father, perhaps with the attendants. Takes make-up and hairbrush for bride with her. At church, she is escorted by an usher to her place in the front left pew.
- Is present at signing of register, and afterwards is escorted by groom's father down aisle.
- Alongside bride's father, stands first in receiving line (if applicable) at reception to greet the guests and thereafter acts as hostess, mixing and introducing guests, etc.
- Afterwards, takes care of bride's wedding dress and accessories, the cake, wedding presents, etc. If the reception is not at home, someone must be responsible for taking home the presents, the top of the cake, the bride and bridegroom's wedding clothes and other items. Those cleaning up should be told who owns what equipment—for example, if cake knives belong to the family or the caterer.
- If reception is at home, directs the clearing-up operation.

The bride's father
- Between the departure of bride's mother for the church and his departure with his daughter, must be a calming influence, supporting and not upsetting the bride in any way.
- Escorts her to the church and down the aisle.
- Gives the bride away.
- Signs the register and then afterwards escorts the groom's mother down the aisle.
- At reception, stands with bride's mother first in the receiving line (if applicable).
- As host, at reception, mixes among guests and introduces them.
- May give the first speech.

The groom

- Gives church fees to the best man so that he can pay them before the ceremony.
- On the wedding morning, gives going-away clothes and honeymoon suitcase to best man, for him to take to the reception venue.
- Gives second speech, in response to the toast to the bride and bridegroom.
- Delivers a stream of thank-yous to the bride's parents, friends who have helped with the catering and flowers, and so on. Proposes a toast to the bridesmaids.
- With help from the best man, has the going-away transport organised for a getaway that is as smooth as possible.

AFTER THE DAY

- Any hired equipment should be returned as soon as possible. **M**.
- Wedding cake should be sent to absent friends. **M**.
- The continuing business of the thank-you letters. Get them over and done with as soon as possible, and don't forget to thank all your helpers—including parents-in-law, relations and friends, caterers, florists, the minister, organist, choir. **B + G**.

Index

Note: Page numbers in *italics* refer to captions.

Acknowledgements

The author and publishers wish to thank the following for permission to reproduce photographs:

Ace Photo Agency: pages 2 photo Roger Howard, 7 photo Mugshots, 10 photo Mugshots, 63 photo Roger Howard, 106 photo Roger Howard; **The Admirable Crichton**: page 42; **Art Directors Photo Library**: pages 17, 116; **Camera Press**: pages 8, 11, 14 photo Ian Swift, 15 photo Snowdon, 36, 52 photo G. Dalla Pozza, 55 photo Geoffrey Shakerley, 64 (above) photo Kent Billequist, 67, 79, 80, 81, 82, 83 photo Terence Donovan, 87, 91, 94, 95, 99 photo Mike Anthony, 104 photo Mike Anthony, 115, 117; **Christie's**, London: page 12; **Lindka Cierach**, designer: page 85; **Crabtree & Evelyn** © Christopher Baker: page 120; **Dumbleton Studios**: wedding of Alex and Leanne Shead, pages 57, 59, 61; **Philip Dumaresq Durell**, photographer: wedding of Louise and Nick Thurlow, pages 3, 22, 40; wedding of Fiona and Robin Illingworth, pages 21, 29, 50 (below); wedding of Katie and Colin McCarraher, pages 31, 108; pages 30, 64 (below), 86, 112; flowers by 'Ring a Ring of Roses' page 141; **Diane Hassall Shoes**: page 93; **Tim Hill**, photographer: page 49; **Impact Photos**: pages 50 (above) photo P. Moulu, 51 photo Mike McQueen; **Landscape Only**: page 25; **Moira Leggat**, photographer: wedding of Gilly and Christopher Stirling, page 32; wedding of Rachel and Nicholas Lane-Fox, page 38; wedding of Jenni and Simon Reekie, page 113; wedding of Cally and James Troup, page 119; and pages 39, 72, 74, 110; **Lonsdale Engraving**: page 47 (right); **Loudoun Papers**: page 47 (left); **Sandra Lousada**, photographer, for Laura Ashley/flowers designed by VASE: front cover, back cover and pages 65, 66, 68, 69, 83, 100 (above), 103; **Sandra Lousada**, photographer, for Image Magazine/flowers designed by VASE: page 90; **Marshall Cavendish** ©: pages 118, 121; **National Magazines/Good Housekeeping**: photos Sandra Lousada, pages 18, 37, 70, 71, 75, 98, 109, 139; **National Magazines/Harpers & Queen**: photo Fabrizio Ferri, page 89. **National Magazines/She Magazine**: photo Eliot Siegel, page 97; **Richard Ogden**, jeweller, page 16; **Rex Features**: pages 35, 41, 45, 53, 100 (below), 101, 102; **Savoy Group**: pages 111, 123; **Mandhir Singh Sethi**, photographer: wedding of Georgie and Mark Rowse, pages 2, 54, 73, 124, 126, 127, 129, 130, 131, 132, 133, 135; wedding of Bella and Nick Hoare, page 19; **Tony Stone Worldwide**: page 33; **Sunday Times Magazine/Lorna Cattel**: pages 76, 78, 105; **Telegraph Colour Library**: page 26 photo John Sims.